"*Spiritual Practices in Community* is a gift to leaders and to the church. With conversational, practical, and down-to-earth wisdom, Diana Shiflett provides a guide for facilitating the practice of ancient and contemporary spiritual disciplines, inviting us to drink deeply from the well of living water together. An experienced leader and pastor, Diana is passionate about helping ministry leaders attend to their own walk with God so they are better equipped to provide space for others to encounter him. I'm grateful for this refreshing and creative spiritual formation resource!"
Sharon Garlough Brown, retreat speaker, author of the Sensible Shoes series

"This is the best how-to resource I know for those who are responsible for guiding others into a deeper experience of the Christian life. The author gives practical step by step instructions on how to lead others (and even yourself) in over thirty spiritual practices in multiple settings and age groups. The book can be used in board meetings, staff meetings, worship services, small groups, children's, youth, and intergenerational ministries, camps, conferences, personal devotions, or even around the dinner table!"
Bradley Nassif, North Park University, author of *Bringing Jesus to the Desert*

"Christian growth is not a solo occupation. It is a partnership between the body of Christ (that's you *and* me) and the Spirit of Christ. The strength of that partnership develops with practice. And this practice, like other practices, can be a team effort. Shiflett highlights how disciplines practiced in community with conversation, questioning, listening, and reflection shape our relationship to God, self, and others. Shiflett is a trustworthy and practical guide. Working from hands-on experience she provides step by step ways to practice spiritual transformation with others."
Adele Calhoun, copastor of spiritual formation, Highrock, Arlington

"As an introvert, I'm constantly amazed at how doing spiritual practices in community is so transforming and so rarely offered. Thank you, Diana, for your excellent coaching and practical ideas!"
Jan Johnson, author of *Meeting God in Scripture* and *Abundant Simplicity*

"Over the years we've learned that spiritual development happens best in relationship—in communion with God together in community. So the focus of this book about encountering God together is exactly what we need in our day. We believe God is inviting leaders to live in divine fullness and others to enjoy this abundant refreshment together. We hope you'll let her very practical book guide you on that very fruitful journey."

Alan Fadling and **Gem Fadling,** founders, Unhurried Living Inc.

"*Spiritual Practices in Community* is an excellent tool for every Christian leader who wants to see people grow in Christ. Pastor Diana Shiflett not only offers engaging experiences to use but also provides the practical guidelines tempered with the voice of wisdom and experience to guide the user. I found this book to be an exciting resource that I can't wait to use and to recommend to other leaders. But I also found it to be a surprising source of spiritual nurture that prompted me to look more closely at my own spiritual practices and challenged me to bring variety to the daily disciplines of my life."

Meagan S. Gillan, director of women ministries, Make and Deepen Disciples Team of the Evangelical Covenant Church

"*Spiritual Practices in Community* takes you on a journey to consider the profound simplicity of being with God. This book will guide you through new experiences to awaken your soul to the presence of God and transform the way you engage with him. There are dozens of simple and refreshing spiritual practices that will help usher you and the community you serve into an intimate experience with God."

Lisa Jarot, vice president for student life, Judson University

SPIRITUAL

PRACTICES

in

COMMUNITY

DRAWING
GROUPS INTO
THE HEART OF GOD

DIANA SHIFLETT

IVP Books

An imprint of InterVarsity Press
Downers Grove, Illinois

InterVarsity Press
P.O. Box 1400, Downers Grove, IL 60515-1426
ivpress.com
email@ivpress.com

InterVarsity Press® is the book-publishing division of InterVarsity Christian Fellowship/ USA®, a movement of students and faculty active on campus at hundreds of universities, colleges, and schools of nursing in the United States of America, and a member movement of the International Fellowship of Evangelical Students. For information about local and regional activities, visit intervarsity.org.

Cover design: David Fassett
Interior design: Jeanna Wiggins
Images: textured blue-green background: © enjoynz / iStock / Getty Images Plus
green leaf: © Avalon_Studio / E+ / Getty Images

ISBN 978-0-8308-4648-1 (print)
ISBN 978-0-8308-7379-1 (digital)

Printed in the United States of America ♾

InterVarsity Press is committed to ecological stewardship and to the conservation of natural resources in all our operations. This book was printed using sustainably sourced paper.

Library of Congress Cataloging-in-Publication Data
A catalog record for this book is available from the Library of Congress.

P 25 24 23 22 21 20 19 18 17 16 15 14 13 12 11 10 9 8 7 6 5 4 3 2 1

Y 37 36 35 34 33 32 31 30 29 28 27 26 25 24 23 22 21 20 19 18

TO THOMAS TEMPLE

(1919–1998)

AKA GRANDDADDY

*In gratitude for the monthly
handwritten letters of encouragement
you sent as I prepared for
and began ministry.*

CONTENTS

GOING DEEPER TOGETHER

Many years ago, as I was reflecting on how I lead, I asked God to reveal his heart to me. An image came to mind: a fountain flowing from above, with me filling a cup and taking the living water to those I was leading. Either I got water too quickly, not allowing the cup to fill, or I spilled it along the way. By the time I got to those I was leading, I no longer had much to share. And I never had enough in my glass to give to all the people I was leading.

In that moment, I realized I needed to change the way I was leading, so I let God continue to reveal things from this image in my mind. *Slow down at the fountain*, I thought. So I walked slowly with my very full cup toward those I was leading.

After that time with God, I took more alone time with him than ever before. And then it hit me: I needed to invite people to stand under the fountain *with me*; I didn't need to tell everyone what they needed to know about God. I started to trust God to speak directly to his people. I also realized I couldn't possibly know everything God wanted to say to every person, but I could introduce them to God. I realized God longs to speak life and truth into everyone's souls—not just mine.

The final image that came to mind was me standing under the flow of Jesus' fountain and inviting others to stand under my cup. My cup was overflowing and so were their cups. In ministry, I found that I no longer had a cup that emptied every time I led a group.

All of our cups are overflowing with what God has for us. My hope for you is that you lead in a new way spiritually, inviting others into the heart of God.

Leading a group in a spiritual practice requires encountering God yourself. Throughout the Scriptures, God encourages his people to draw near to him. He invites us to come and drink living waters without cost (Isaiah 55:1). And Jesus interrupted a festival to say, "Come drink the living waters."

> On the last and greatest day of the festival, Jesus stood and said in a loud voice, "Let anyone who is thirsty come to me and drink. Whoever believes in me, as Scripture has said, rivers of living water will flow from within them." By this he meant the Spirit, whom those who believed in him were later to receive. Up to that time the Spirit had not been given, since Jesus had not yet been glorified. (John 7:37-39)

We live in a thirsty world that's looking to leaders to lead well. This book is an opportunity to learn to lead differently. It will help you to not only tell people about the living water that Christ has to offer but also invite them to experience the thirst-quenching Spirit of Jesus Christ for themselves alongside you.

Over the years I've served as a pastor, I've heard these three statements often:

■ "I am not feeling fed at church."

■ "Thank you for your sermon today!"

■ "Christ is transforming my life."

If you're like me, you hear the first two phrases far more than you hear the last. Yet we do ministry so that people will be transformed spiritually. I'd much rather people tell me their lives are being transformed spiritually than hear the first two phrases.

Simply put, spiritual practices are different ways of connecting with God. Over twenty-three years of ministry, I've gotten in a rhythm of using them. They have transformed me and the ministries I'm a part of. When I'm living into the practices and using them well as I lead, I feel fully alive in Christ— and often so do the people around me.

When I teach about spiritual practices, listeners often ask how they can lead the practices themselves in their own ministry contexts. We usually take a few moments right then and there to discuss different ideas, but a few minutes is not enough. People need more than a quick conversation; they need a book. My hope is that *Spiritual Practices in Community* gives you what you need to lead certain practices well in your context. Since everyone's context is different, you'll need to adjust each practice to fit yours.

Over the years, spiritual practices often have been referred to as spiritual disciplines. Some date back to the Old Testament, such as fasting and prayer. Others were created and refined during the hundreds of centuries of church history. Some of the ones in this book I've created along the way. Others I've learned from partners in ministry.

Each person is wired differently, and spiritual practices give us different ways to engage with God, according to how we best connect with him. In this book, you'll find more than thirty different ways to engage with God. Encourage a group you're in or leading to try different practices that may help them connect with God.

HELPING INDIVIDUALS AND GROUPS ENGAGE

Sometimes people assume they won't like an activity because they didn't like it in a different context. A woman in one of my spiritual practices groups said she didn't like to journal. I said, "Just try it in class when we're together, and you'll never have to do it again." Months later, she told the class she loved it.

There's something about connecting with God in new ways; it can awaken our souls. When we focus on listening to and talking to God, mundane things can suddenly have life. Recently I taught a class of first through sixth graders. First I asked them to draw what I was reading from the Scriptures. One third grader chimed in right away and said, "I don't like to draw."

"Do you like to write?" I asked.

"No," she said.

"Okay, well, how about you just try, and I will try too, and we'll see what happens," I answered.

She agreed, and as I read, I drew some terrible pictures. Seeing what I was doing, the whole class started to draw and to write. As we finished the practice, I asked her how she liked it, and she said, "It was kinda fun." All the children were given time to show their picture to the group and share what they'd learned about God.

Almost every time I lead a practice, and no matter what age I lead, some don't want to participate. I validate their feelings and request their engagement or silence. It seems the quicker I validate and encourage the group, the better it goes for everyone.

At the end, sometimes someone still feels it wasn't a good practice. I acknowledge that and say that it's good to learn what works and doesn't work for us so we can connect with God in ways that are best for us.

There's a time and a place for traditional messages and sermons, but there also need to be places where we listen for the voice of God together. As leaders, we need to start making more space for spiritual practices to help people learn how to meet and experience God. It's important that we live into ways in which *we* are connecting with and hearing from God so we can lead and teach others to do the same.

You can't lead where you aren't willing to go. As a leader, I experience spiritual growth when I lead practices. I learn from others as we share what God is doing in each of us. Because of this, I hope that as you move through this book, you experience God for yourself and then lead others in these practices so they too can enter into the presence of God. I give you full permission to do what we have all done in ministry: jump into a particular spiritual practice that you need to lead right now— whether it's for your edification or for those you will lead. My prayer and hope for you is that you will go and be with God yourself first. I hope you long for spiritual practice spaces—and find them. The best moments in leadership for me have come from experiencing God before I led a group.

USING *SPIRITUAL PRACTICES IN COMMUNITY*

The first chapter of this book shows how to lead spiritual practices in general. The rest of the chapters lay out how to lead more than thirty different practices (and in the back of the book, you'll find an alphabetical list of every practice in the book, with corresponding page numbers). Each chapter includes spiritual practices, and each practice can be used in multiple settings with multiple age groups. I'll explain how you can do each spiritual practice yourself and then how you can lead the practice.

Each practice works well with any size group. You'll also find several examples of how you as a spiritual leader can use a specific spiritual practice in different arenas, such as in worship, meetings, or ministry to adults or children, and also in your own family and your own life. Some of these practices can even help you experience more intimacy in your marriage.

As you read, let these ideas be springboards for finding creative ways to help those you lead to enter deeply into a relationship with Jesus Christ. Don't feel you have to do the practices exactly the way I present them. Because only you know your context, let the practices come alive as you lead in the way God is calling you to lead.

LEADING SPIRITUAL PRACTICES

OVER THE PAST TEN YEARS, I've shared leadership with others at a winter retreat. One of my favorite moments was when I was watching another pastor learn on the fly. We had a group of two hundred people in the room, and I had written the script he was to read. It included him encouraging individuals to share spiritually and deeply with the person next to them about their lives. As you can imagine, after two minutes of two hundred people talking, the noise level had risen considerably.

The sound system wasn't working, and without thinking, the young pastor yelled at the top of his lungs, "Hey!" Suddenly the room went silent—until he and I burst out laughing. Through his uncontrollable laughter, he said, "I guess that wasn't my best soothing spiritual voice." He held up his hand with his pointer and pinky up and the rest of the fingers folded down and confidently said, "From now on, when I'm pulling us back together, I'll raise my hand like this, and you imitate it so others know it's time to be quiet, because this is Quiet Giraffe."

I loved how he handled that moment. He was able to laugh at himself and draw the group back after a yell. He quickly regrouped and moved forward to finish the spiritual practice well. When you're leading and something unexpected happens, it's okay to laugh, regroup, and move forward. That day I learned that a spiritual practice is more than the script.

When used corporately, spiritual practices help to grow people deeply in Christ as well as with one another. They create a way—and a space—to hear the voice of God together.

LEADING SPIRITUAL PRACTICES

Teaching spiritual practices is one of the best ways I've found to help propel a group forward. The group grows in its spiritual depth and in its relationships spiritually.

You can lead practices in various locations and groups:

- board meetings
- staff meetings
- worship services
- small groups
- mission trips
- prayer rooms
- retreats
- youth ministries
- children's ministries
- intergenerational ministries
- camps
- conferences
- around the dinner table
- during devotions

If at all possible, do a spiritual practice on your own before you lead it, even if it's a shortened form done quickly because you're about to lead the practice. It's worth taking the time to experience it yourself. This will make you more capable of talking about the process and will give you the ability to share how you met God in the practice. You'll also be able to talk about what was hard about the experience.

Doing it on your own at least once helps you with three things. First, you can share your experiences, good or bad. As you're doing a practice on your own, take a few notes about what God reveals to you as you listen for his voice. Don't limit what you write in this moment; you won't have to share everything you write down. Some moments between you and God are intimate and can help you understand why someone would choose not to share in a group.

Second, if you haven't done it yourself, it's hard to know how much silence is too long or too short to hear from God. Others have led me in spiritual practices, and when they've done it themselves beforehand, I can tell. The amount of silence seems right on target.

Third, meeting with God before you invite others into a time with God is extremely helpful for your personal spiritual well-being. All too often people in ministry forget to make sure they're feeding their own souls so they can help others. When I was training in ministry, we were reminded throughout the process that we couldn't take anyone where we weren't willing and able to go ourselves. If you aren't willing to go to the depths with God in preparation for leading a practice, you won't know how to take others there. Remind yourself of this truth as you explore each chapter.

When I first started taking time to meet with God before teaching others, no matter how hard I tried, I was unable to quiet my mind for fear I'd forget to do something important later in the day. So I kept a small piece of paper next to me to write down what came to mind. I wouldn't have realized how distracting the need to vacuum can be if I hadn't slowed myself down to meet with God. Experiencing what those you lead may experience is invaluable.

SET UP THE ROOM

I do spiritual practices in all sorts of settings with different numbers of people. If I'm leading a group of more than ten, it's very helpful to divide them into smaller groups that stay in one room. If I'm leading a group of more than ten, I like to set up the room with round tables with four to six people per table. Try to keep the same number of people at each table so you can all finish at about the same time.

However, I don't always have the luxury of setting up a room of round tables, so when I arrive, I assess what my game plan will be for discussions. I decide if people will move their chairs and face one another. If they're in pews or rows of chairs, I decide if I'll encourage them to turn to talk to someone behind or in front of them or have them turn to a person next to them. Think about this before you are in the moment. Also guide people very specifically so little time is lost.

If you encourage participants to talk to someone in the same pew, they'll likely be talking to someone they know. If you encourage them to turn around, they'll likely know that person less or not at all. As you think about which way to have people turn, consider what your goals are. Do you want people to go deeper in relationship, or do you want them to connect with those they don't know? Either is fine, but know what your goal is before you start.

If writing is part of the practice, you'll need to have tables or other hard surfaces to write on. If participants won't be writing, a circle without a table is another great way to set up the space. A circle allows everyone to face one another and be on the same level. When discussion is happening, everyone in the circle needs to be able to make eye contact and to hear each other. Take time at the beginning to make sure these can happen. Hearing and seeing are key, since everyone's words are valuable to the group.

CREATE SPACE THAT'S NOT JUST PHYSICAL

You want people to be able to enter in, so you need to help them hold the space with God. This means both keeping track of the time and making sure you are guiding the time at the level they need and can handle. Let the group know the overall concept of the spiritual practice and that you will be the time keeper as you lead them through each step. For example, stating how long you will hold the silence and suggesting ways participants can be present to God helps them hold the space well.

Try to understand what a group can withstand and for how long. For example, you can hold times of silence longer with spiritual directors than with teenagers or children. Also, don't find the level they're comfortable with; find one they can handle. When we're growing in our faith, we're rarely comfortable. Seek a level of risk that's right on the growing edge for that particular group. Also tell the group how long the silence will be each time. For teens, one to five minutes can feel like an eternity. For spiritual directors, it can feel too short. Try hard to stick close to the time you promised the group. When you stick to that time, you gain trust with them.

Remember that people are always thinking about something. When leading a spiritual practice, one important goal is to create space so people can stop thinking about distractions and give space for God's voice to be heard. Keeping things on time helps people not worry about their schedule. When you promise they'll have time to ask questions, make sure you hold to that time. Then when you promise you'll let them out on time, they'll know they don't need to watch the clock.

However, also follow the Holy Spirit. If the Spirit wants more time with a group, look for ways to let some people slip out of the room, if needed. It isn't life-giving when a leader tries to hold a group until they all hear the voice of God. Those sitting under your leadership who have tight schedules need the freedom to go.

At the end of each practice, get feedback from participants by asking how they're doing and how you're doing in your leadership role. That way, each time you lead a spiritual practice, you get to hone your leadership skills.

BREATHE DEEPLY

While a friend of mine was in the Pediatric Intensive Care Unit with her little girl, she read this on a sign: "Breathing deeply resets your nervous system." Breathing deeply is also one of the easiest ways to deal with anxiety. Consider doing it before you start or at any moment when you need to reset yourself during a spiritual practice. Also, one of the best gifts you can give those you lead is a genuine space of calm as you lead. When people sense that you're calm, they feel calm. When you're full of anxiety, most people can hear it in your voice and will internalize it, even if they don't realize they're taking on your anxiety.

Therapists teach people who struggle with anxiety to do four-count breathing. This practice can be good for you as you lead and for those you're leading. Also consider having participants breathe deeply with you at the opening of each spiritual practice. This can help them focus on their breathing instead of all the other things distracting them. It's a great way to start a meeting and a great way to remember that God is the one who breathes life into us; each breath is a gift from him. You can even remind the group of that truth. After you teach breath prayer to a group (see chapter four), you can add it to the beginning of each practice you teach.

LISTEN FOR THE HOLY SPIRIT

As you start any of the spiritual practices, pause and invite the Holy Spirit to speak. Also ask the Holy Spirit to speak to the people you're leading as well as to be at work in you as you speak, lead, and teach. Pray this prayer out loud, or simply pray it as you're breathing deeply before you start teaching. Set your heart and mind to desire to hear from God as you lead.

Another way to stay aware of the Holy Spirit is to light a candle. In fact, most spiritual directors light a candle in their sessions. The movement of the flame of the candle can remind you that the Spirit is moving and active in the room. Feel free to let people know why you're lighting it, so they too can stay aware of the movement of the Spirit throughout the spiritual practice. Instruct them that looking at the candle can also help them refocus on the Spirit when distracted.

BE YOURSELF

A good goal for the first time you lead a spiritual practice is not to chase your group away from spiritual practices permanently. People know if you're being anything but authentic. Feel free to be creative by morphing the spiritual practices in this book into your own style. Enjoy being created in the image of the great Creator by being creative yourself. If you don't do the practice yourself first, the group will know you're just reading off a script. If you don't make it your own, it won't go smoothly. If needed to take the pressure off being perfect, call it an experiment.

Let people know who you are without adding commentary as you lead. Share only what is real and true for you and what is directly connected to the practice. If what I've written regarding a practice doesn't sound like you, restate it in your own words—unless they are from the Word of God, of course.

LEAD, DON'T PREACH

Once you've started a spiritual practice, make sure you're not preaching and instead are facilitating a space where people can meet with Jesus. Make sure each of your words is used to take people deeper into the practice rather than into a space where they're taking in factual information from you rather than what God has to say to them. It's great to teach people about God, but it's important to make sure you're creating a space for others to meet with God. If you know you're good at preaching or teaching, do that before or after the practice; don't interrupt God as he's speaking to his people. I remind myself that God is in the middle of a personal sermon for each person in the room, and that sermon will be more powerful than anything I could ever say. It's a much higher honor to lead people into a space to meet with the living God than to tell them how they can meet him.

Sometimes people tell me about their experience in group spiritual practice, and in the middle of the story, one of us realizes I was the one leading the practice. I know I've led well when the participants don't remember I was leading. The moment is about God, not the facilitator. This reality keeps me in check. If this whole idea makes you feel resistant, God may have some soul work for you to do before you start leading others into his presence.

Take a moment to lean back from these words and talk to God about how you want to be known as a great leader, or maybe how you'd rather not be a great leader—or a leader at all. Let him speak words of affirmation over you. Let him remind you that he wants to do a mighty work in and through you. He needs your ego to step back.

God does want to use you; he wants all of us to be a part of his great work. But we must remember that it's his work, not ours. Trust me; even in the process of writing this book, I've had to let go of me being the creator. God is the great Creator, and I am created in his image so I can be creative. I can't take his place.

DON'T RUSH

As you're leading a spiritual practice, do your best not to rush the process. Sometimes this means being silent in front of a crowd longer than you're comfortable. Speak slowly, concisely, and gently. Leave time and space for you to hear the Holy Spirit and for those you're leading to hear too. Also be aware that some people in the room may be hard of hearing; you may have to be louder than you think.

There will be moments when you're tempted to race ahead, maybe because you're worried nothing is happening in people or maybe they're getting antsy or too quiet. It can feel scary to keep a slow pace, and you may fear running out of time. This is why doing the practice before you lead it is important; you get a feel for how long each piece takes.

If there's another leader in the room, I usually pick up that person's anxiety. He or she may be the person that hired me to lead a retreat or the senior pastor in the sponsoring church or even the power player who has no problem voicing his or her opinion during or after the practice. Try to follow God's prompting in the moment, not the feelings of a disruptive person in the room. Trust that God has a plan, and do your best to follow him in those moments.

Whether you're reading out loud or talking, it's important to speak slowly. Slowing down will help you hear the Holy Spirit, even as you're leading. Sometimes this means speaking like you are the Amplified Version of the Bible, saying something two or three ways that mean the same thing, to help people understand what you're saying. As you lead, God may add something to your sentence you don't expect.

By slowing your speech, you give space to yourself and others to hear from the Holy Spirit. We all need that space. When we speak quickly, it's hard for people to engage both with our words and with what God is prompting. You're taking people to a place where they're listening to three different voices simultaneously: theirs, yours, and God's. If you speak quickly, they can avoid the deep place with God and hear only you.

The first thing your listeners are taking in is your voice, so they need to be able to understand what you've said. Once they've heard and comprehended, they'll then be able to check in with their own internal voice. After they've heard those two levels, they can hear the still small voice of God.

This all happens almost simultaneously. If you move too fast, they'll get stuck just trying to hear and understand your voice. They'll miss checking in with themselves, making it impossible for them to hear from God. When we speak slowly, we can hear more too. We aren't just giving people information that they're writing in their notebooks.

The first time you do this, it will feel painfully slow. Let that happen. When you're finished, ask your group about your pacing. Often people want more silence in the process than you'd expect.

USE A TIMER

As you move through each piece of a spiritual practice, put your phone on silent and ask your listeners to do the same. This will give you, them, and God some good space. Yet even a phone on silent during a spiritual practice can be distracting. I have been in a room where someone's phone in their purse just seems to keep vibrating, and the owner does not attend to it, but several other people in the room keep looking toward the purse. For myself, I have gotten distracted by a text that comes in as I'm leading. Even though no one else knows about it, instead of being present to the Holy Spirit and the people in the room, I'm suddenly elsewhere mentally and spiritually. I will sometimes say that as we put our phones into airplane mode, it may cause anxiety at first because we are disconnecting from people outside the room, but that it will give us good space to connect with God and others inside the room.

Before you start, decide how many minutes you want to give to each part of the practice so you don't run out of time before the end of each. The last part of a practice—debriefing with the whole group—is important. When we debrief well, the whole group gains spiritually and is unified spiritually.

Some leaders like to use a gentle alarm or vibration on their phone to let the group know time is up. I like to use my voice, since even a gentle alarm causes some people to think it's time to burst out talking about how hard it was to be in silence, jarring those who enjoyed the silence. If you use your voice, it gives space to instruct people in that moment as well.

Depending on your group, you may need to instruct them how to come out of silence. Some spiritual directors will stay quiet with their eyes closed for as long as you let them, and some middle school students blurt something out as soon as the time is up. Leading with your voice encourages people to go where you're headed next rather than to start a free-for-all.

Another important aspect to remember when leading spiritual practices is that at least one person is watching the clock.

Sometimes they're watching it because they know they have to leave at a certain time. Other clock watchers are just waiting for the class to be over. Be aware of this, because even one person can sway the whole group in the wrong direction if given the opportunity.

The key to letting the Spirit lead is to respect everyone's time. By starting and ending on time, you have a better chance of God breaking through to even the controllers in the room. This leads us into the next step.

GET TO KNOW YOUR AUDIENCE

If you're working with a group you don't know, ask a person who knows the group well to tell you about it. If you're leading a large gathering, do your research by looking it up online, and use language similar to what they use on their website. When I'm going to a location where I don't know anyone, I arrive at least thirty minutes to an hour early. During that time, I do my best to learn a few names before we get started. If I can, I ask them a few questions to get a general idea of who's in the room before we start. When we know people's names, we have the ability to engage them specifically. I'm not suggesting calling on people, but when they raise their hand or start to talk, you can address them by name. Using names also helps the whole group feel more connected and warm.

STAY IN TUNE WITH YOUR AUDIENCE

While you're leading, take time to notice people's facial expressions. If you see looks of confusion, rephrase what you just said. Also use different examples to help people understand concepts.

If you've asked the group to write, when about half the people have stopped writing, move the practice along. Some people will write until you tell them to stop, but others will write only what you've guided them to document in that moment. When those people are done, they may start thinking about something else, so help the whole group stay with what God is doing by noticing who is done and moving on to the next task at hand.

Are participants crying? Crying during a spiritual practice can be a sign that the Holy Spirit is present and that he's doing a deep work in that person's soul. When I see or hear crying, I remind the group it's okay to cry. I add that often it's because of a deep work happening inside, so it's good to let the tears flow. I try to make it sound like a general announcement, not directed at a specific person. One time after I did this, someone came to me and said, "Right when you gave us permission to cry, I had just started crying. I was so thankful you said it, so I could trust God was at work." When we notice this movement but don't name it, participants are likely to focus on trying not to cry rather than leaning into the work God is doing inside them.

Use humor as well. I do this in my introductions so skeptics know I can be fun—and so can God. However, if you tend to overuse humor, do your best to keep it in check while leading the spiritual practice so people aren't distracted from what God is doing. Create a space for them to be still and to know he is God. Also, if you feel uncomfortable with people expressing emotions, try not to interrupt with a misplaced joke. Humor is best used to put others at ease, not you as the leader.

Watch body language in the room. If people are falling asleep, pick up the pace. If people are sitting with their arms crossed, build trust with them, for instance by using humor. Chat a little bit with the group, and let them ask you a few questions about you if they seem distant. Ask them a few questions about themselves too. In the beginning of a session with youth, I first ask a question or two that everyone knows the answer to so everyone gets to speak at least once. This allows them to feel free to say something.

Ask God to give you eyes to see what he wants you to see and ears to hear what you need to hear. Sometimes a spiritual practice will fall flat, or participants have a hard time engaging with certain ones. This is normal and okay. Address it in real time so people continue to try other spiritual practices, even if the first one or two didn't go well. I say things like, "Sometimes the first time you do a spiritual practice it's uncomfortable. These are spiritual *practices* because we're practicing connecting with God. Just like anything we practice, we get better and better the more we practice." I also usually add something like, "You may never like some spiritual practices, and it's okay." I encourage people to try everything once or twice, and I let them know if it doesn't work for them, they don't need to keep doing it. I remind them, "These practices are to help you connect with God, not to frustrate you."

DEBRIEF WELL

Debriefing gives the gift of hearing how God moved during a spiritual practice. When we have a powerful moment with God, the impressions it provides can fade quickly. We may even question that it happened at all. Verbalizing what God said soon after the moment brings it into reality. It helps us realize and remember what God spoke clearly.

The best questions to ask in the debriefing are open ended. An open-ended question cannot be answered with a simple yes or no. You are looking for the group to share about what God said and did during the spiritual practice. You need questions that will draw out what they just experienced with God. Not every question has to be connected to God, but do ask that kind of question if you notice no one is focusing on God. It sometimes helps to ask a God question after you've asked a few process questions to warm up the group; most people need to have a certain level of trust before they'll share from the heart.

Here are a few questions that can be used with just about any spiritual practice:

- What was this process like for you?
- What was hard about this process?
- What did you enjoy about this process?
- What felt significant to you during the spiritual practice?
- What did you hear God saying? What do you think God was saying to *you*?
- Did any Scripture come to mind while we were doing the practice?
- Did you find yourself focusing on an attribute of God?
- What do you feel God is inviting you toward in your life now?

When you debrief the group, help them listen to each other, and encourage everyone to share something. I often have participants share with a smaller group before they share with the large group. This especially helps introverts. You're teaching the group how to have spiritual conversations not only at the time but also later.

Debriefing helps people articulate their encounter with Christ. Doing it as a group gives them the ability to engage with one another about what God is doing, and they're more likely to keep engaging with each other. This part of the process is also very important if someone had a strong negative or emotional experience.

God also calls us to walk through pain together. As Scripture says, "Mourn with those who mourn" (Romans 12:15). It's a privilege to carry one another's burdens. Together we can bring them to God, for he desires to carry our burdens for us. Christ longs to grant his peace to his people, and he uses people to minister to each other so that he may be glorified.

PRACTICING SILENCE *with* OTHERS

Silence is the absence of noise. When we find a way to quiet our exterior world, our interior world can become quiet enough for us to experience the presence of God. The idea of practicing silence *together* may seem counterintuitive, but silence when others are present can be even more palpable than when alone.

One of the easiest ways to help people engage in a silence filled with the presence of God is by doing a simple two-minute silence exercise. The first time I tried this, it was with middle school students, and the results were stunning. I told the students I was going to give them one minute of full silence to think about anything they wanted to. When the time was up, I broke the silence by asking the group to share the things they were thinking about. One of them immediately said, "I was thinking about if it would be okay to think dirty thoughts at church. But I never got to the point of thinking dirty thoughts, because I was just thinking about if it would be okay."

Doing all I could to be the professional adult I was supposed to be, I simply nodded and thanked him for sharing so honestly. But inside I was holding back laughter. I loved this moment, because the student felt comfortable to engage the experience honestly and say what was going on in his mind. He had engaged with the spiritual practice fully.

Continuing with the experience, I had them take the next minute to focus on God. This time, as my luck would have it, our youth room mascot, a hamster named Winnie the Pooh, got loose and began scampering around the room. I chased him back and forth for the majority of what was supposed to be the God-focused sixty seconds before I caught him and returned him to his cage. Much to my surprise, as we exited that exciting minute of silence, the students held the silence—even after me chasing Pooh. That minute taught me a lot about preparing people to stay silent no matter what happens.

I had prepared these students because I knew that, given the opportunity, they would use silence to be funny. I did it by encouraging them to listen closely to see if God had something to say to them personally. In an attempt to draw the focus away from the hamster fiasco, I asked, "Besides thinking about me chasing the hamster, what did you think during the second minute of silence?" This invited them to move past the distraction and to tell the group how God had met them. The shockingly honest young man spoke up again, saying that hearing from God was more important in the second minute—a decision I trust was a blessing to him after his challenging first minute.

Adult settings have different distractions. People arrive late, leave early, and walk out to go to the bathroom, get a cup of coffee, or answer their phones. When I prepare adult groups, I ask them to help one another hear from God by holding the silence for the time we've agreed on as a group. Each of us sees silence differently, and making that clear at the beginning helps the whole group hold the silence.

Usually a couple of people believe they're still holding the silence if they're whispering to someone about God. If I think one or two people may do this, I offer to be the person they process with or ask questions of during longer times of silence. This helps protect the gift of silence for the rest of the group.

All people experience silence differently. Some are very uncomfortable in silence, and not knowing when it will end makes it worse. Some people love silence and can sit in it for days on end. These people may have anxiety when you end the silence before they're ready.

For middle school students, I usually hold the silence for one minute at most. Go much past a minute, and you can almost guarantee inappropriate noises—or a hamster—will ruin the moment. As you practice silence with them, they can handle more and more time. High school students can start with two minutes if clearly guided about what they are to focus on.

With adults, when there are more than six in the room, usually five minutes is the maximum. The more people in the room, the more difficult it becomes for everyone to stay silent—unless they're doing something like journaling or drawing. Eventually someone coughs or a cell phone buzzes, which shifts the attention from the internal to the external for those in the room.

It's best to keep the time condensed and focused. People try harder to keep the silence if they know it's limited. One exception to this rule is when working with spiritual directors and others who already practice silence. They can easily be silent in a guided experience for fifteen to twenty minutes.

Make sure you tell every group how long you'll be holding the silence, and then stick to that amount of time.

THE SPIRITUAL AND BIBLICAL
PERSPECTIVE ON SILENCE

At the beginning of Christ's ministry, he took forty days to fast and pray. It's hard to fathom anyone doing this, but silence and solitude are extremely important for those who are called to ministry. Christ was alone for forty days, devoting all his energy to prayer and connection to the Father. He took those forty days right before he started his public ministry. I would love to have heard his thoughts during those days.

We do get a glimpse into Jesus' time of solitude in Matthew 4:1-11, when we see the three ways he responded to temptation. Each time he was tempted, he responded with God's Word, quoting Scripture and relying on its truth and power. We too can take time to be silent before the Lord, fighting off the temptations we experience. It's good for us to rely on God's Word as Jesus modeled for us.

Many things in life can pull us away from the heart of God, and sometimes we need to take times of silence with the Lord to reset ourselves and to realize just how much power the world has over us. Silence can help us see what's vying for our time and attention. In silence, we can choose to claim the Word of God instead of remaining blind due to the lack of attention we're giving to God.

Jesus often pulled away to pray. "Very early in the morning, while it was still dark, Jesus got up, left the house and went off to a solitary place, where he prayed" (Mark 1:35). The fact that he needed time to be alone to hear God's voice is a helpful reminder to us that we too need time to pause and listen for the voice of God so we can move in the direction he's calling us. I'm thankful we can read in the book of Luke that Jesus made a point to withdraw often: "Jesus often withdrew to lonely places and prayed" (Luke 5:16). This means that I too, as a follower of Christ, need to make sure to withdraw *often*.

MY THOUGHTS VERSUS GOD'S THOUGHTS

I love to lead busy adults in an exercise on sitting in silence. It helps us understand how to sit in a peaceful stance with God rather than in the worry-filled, task-oriented silence we get stuck in a majority of the time. When I do this practice, in the first minute of silence, most participants reflect on what they feel they should be doing instead of being still. During debriefing, they often say that first minute stirred up a long to-do list or a reviewing of their schedules. Others were worrying about the people they cared for. Sometimes they felt like jumping out of their skin by the time the minute ended, because it seemed so incredibly long.

For adults, the beautiful part of the exercise tends to happen in the second minute. Many remark on how peaceful it felt and how short. Some take the second minute to visualize spending time with Jesus. One of my favorite stories is of a person who imagined being outside on a beautiful day, swinging on a porch swing, experiencing the love of Christ. At other times, people weep because they were still for the first time in a long time, experiencing God's presence. Others enter a deep time of relaxation as they let Jesus hold all their stress and anxiety.

This exercise is simple and is best done any time you want to use spiritual practices that require silence. We live in a world that no longer *does* silence very well or very often. Therefore, it's a fast way to experience the difference between human silence and the God-driven silence Jesus experienced.

Take one minute to think about whatever you want.
Take a second minute to focus on God.

Leading My Thoughts Versus God's Thoughts

With very little preparation the first time you lead this exercise, simply get your timer out and tell the group, "We are going to practice silence together for two minutes." Tell them that for the first minute you will set the timer, and they can think about whatever they want.

If you're using a timer on a phone or tablet, consider using a loud alarm as a way of contrasting the stillness of the silence with the loud world we live in. It's fun to use a popular ringtone to help them connect the concept of how little silence we experience with how quickly the loud things in our lives tempt us and distract us from being able to use our brains simply to think.

Take the following steps to complete the practice:

- Set your timer and say, "Go."

- Break the silence after exactly one minute. Ask, "Is anyone willing to share what they thought about for that minute?" Ask them to try to tell how that minute felt in just a sentence or two.

- Let two to five people share for about thirty seconds each. Encourage those that share to do it in one or two sentences so you can move to the second minute. The primary goal of this first minute is to show how uncomfortable we tend to feel when we're left to sit within our own mind.

- Thank people as they share, and try not to comment much beyond that. Affirm them so they feel more confident to share again when asked to respond to deeper, more challenging thoughts. Thanking people for their honesty can be helpful long term. Sometimes repeating what a participant says can ensure that the whole group heard and can make that person feel validated and heard.

- After a few people have shared, let the group know you're going to take one more minute to sit in the presence of God. This time, ask them to try to focus on God instead of their thoughts. Give them helpful tips: "You may picture yourself actually sitting with God. You may talk to each other, or you may just tell God you're listening and then listen to see what he has to say. Some people like to go someplace special with God. Enjoy this moment in time with God."

- Encourage the group to sit comfortably and take a deep breath before beginning.

- Open the time with a short prayer, asking God to let the group get present with him.

- Set your timer for one minute, not using a loud alarm this time. I usually use the stopwatch in my phone instead of the alarm.

- When the minute is up, pray gently to end the time of silence. Thank God for letting you sit in his presence. Ask if anyone is willing to share what God did during that minute. Ask how that second minute felt different from the first minute.

Once you've led this practice with a group, they're ready to try other forms of silence. Warming them up with a small silence exercise like this also helps you understand the level of silence the group can tolerate. Perhaps more importantly, it can prepare them to sit in silence more. You've taught them by *doing* rather than by *telling* them how. And hopefully they'll choose to do this practice more often.

You've given them space that likely no one else is going to give them. By having them try silence together in a crowded room, you've brought normalcy to the whole group as well as permission to be with God instead of on their phones every time they have a spare moment. This could be the new way they use their time when standing in line, waiting for a bus, or during other times in a day when waiting happens.

PALMS UP, PALMS DOWN

I first learned about Palms Up, Palms Down in college when reading Richard Foster's *Celebration of Discipline*. This simple prayer practice is an excellent way to focus on the presence of God.

Often when we sit down to read Scripture or to listen to a sermon, we become lost in our thoughts and distractions. It's hard to shift gears and listen for the voice of God instead of our racing thoughts. Palms Up, Palms Down is a great way to let go of distractions and hard situations so you can engage with the living God. I encourage you to try this as you begin a time of worship or a sermon, or when starting some other spiritual practice. This practice can be done quickly, or you can take as long as you'd like to let your heart focus on God, not on your circumstances.

Here is how you begin:

- As you sit, plant both feet on the floor in front of you.
- Close your eyes.
- Take a few deep breaths, and relax your mind and body.
- Place both hands in your lap, one on each thigh, or even hovering above your legs if you'd like.

Say something like this:

- As your hands are palms down, think about it as letting go of anything you're holding on to that's distracting you from God. Release anything that's stressful. If something or someone has hurt you, see if you can picture yourself letting it go, allowing it to drop to the floor. Maybe even imagine yourself dropping your anxiety into the hands of Christ, at the foot of the cross, or at the feet of Jesus sitting on the throne. Use whatever image works best for you.

- Try to find a clear way to "watch" those distracting thoughts fall out of your hands. Relax as you're dropping them, and remind yourself that Jesus longs to take care of them for you. Let yourself feel him taking these burdens from your hands, and acknowledge that he can handle them.

- After you've let go of as much as you can let go of, flip your hands over, palms up. At this moment, let God know you want to receive what he has to offer you. Let Jesus share with you what he wants to give you. Open your hands, and lift them higher as a way of saying, "I want what you have to offer me today."

- As soon as you find your mind wandering, flip your palms downward and drop the distracting thought as fast as you can in order to get your focus back to God. So often we miss what God has as we're distracting ourselves with worry.

- Flip your hands back and forth as many times as needed to release all the stress you've put on yourself—or seemingly people have put on you. Let yourself receive from God all that he has to offer you in that moment.

This spiritual practice is not only helpful corporately, as everyone in the room is doing it together, but it's also helpful when you're struggling to fall asleep at night or as you enter into alone time with God.

On your own before you lead

Palms down, let go of all your distractions.
Palms up, receive what God has to offer you.

Leading Palms Up, Palms Down

Lead the group by saying something like this:

- Get comfortable in your seats.

- Put your hands palm-down on your lap.

- Now raise them so they're hovering just above your legs. Think about the things that are distracting you, and imagine your hands releasing these things and letting them drop.

- Feel free to close your eyes so you can imagine this happening.

- As your hands feel empty, flip them over in a posture of receiving what God has for you.

- Offer God a prayer, telling him you're open to receive whatever he has to give you today.

- Go back and forth between these two postures as many times as you need throughout our time together.

CENTERING PRAYER

Spending two minutes in silence and some time doing Palms Up, Palms Down sets your group up perfectly to try another silence exercise. Centering prayer is a much deeper and more focused time of prayer. It involves a twenty-minute time of silence with the goal of resting in the presence of God and was created as an update of contemplative prayer practices that have been around for centuries.

The first time I did centering prayer, I was told to think of a word to focus on during twenty minutes of silence. My class-mates seemed unfazed by the fact that the leader had just asked us to focus on *one* word for *twenty* minutes. Everyone around the circle closed their eyes, so I did too. Then the longest twenty minutes of my life ensued.

First, I thought, *I'm committed to the process. I want to do the practice well. I'm an adult in a seminary class. I've been leading in ministry for years. I can do this.*

As we started, my mind found the word *joy.* I thought, *Joy is a lovely concept. I would love to spend twenty minutes dwelling on joy.* But then I remembered I was focusing on only one word, not on a concept. So I made my mind just think about the word by repeating the word *joy* in my head over and over again. *Joy, joy, joy.* Suddenly I found myself singing in my head, *Down in my heart, down in my heart,* and then in Spanish, *Yo tengo gozo gozo gozo gozo en me corazón, en me corazón. Wait, wait, wait, I do not think this is what she wanted us to be doing.*

So I tried again, thinking, *Maybe if I said it slower in my head, I would feel more joyful. Joooooooooyyyy, joooooyyy, jooooooy.*

About a minute and a half into this practice, I thought I'd better change words, since *joy* wasn't working for me. I thought, *I don't feel any more joyful than two minutes ago, and I still have eighteen minutes on the clock.* Everyone else around the circle seemed at peace. *That's it!* I thought. *Peace. Peace, peace, peace, peace. . . . Now I'm stressed out. I'm feeling the opposite of what this practice is supposed to offer.* By the end of the twenty minutes, I thought I might explode.

Eight years later, I decided to try it again on my own to see if it was something I could lead others in. I thought, *It must be a good practice. People have been doing it for many years.* As I thought about leading it in a group, I knew I didn't understand the concept of centering prayer. So I started doing some research to see if I could understand it enough as a trained spiritual director.

Within ten minutes, I had one of those aha moments and was ready to love this practice for all it had to offer. The main concept is to pick a word or image so when you aren't resting in God's presence during the twenty minutes of silence, you use the word or image to draw you back into his presence. The leader during my first experience probably had said this, but I may have heard only that we would be in a room with twenty people for twenty minutes without talking.

It may surprise you to know that I'm an extrovert who now loves to live into her inner introvert. But at the time, I thought, *What a waste of perfectly good people time!*

This spiritual practice does not work well with most people under eighteen. I was in my thirties when I first tried it, and I didn't get it until I was in my forties. Of course, there are a few children who can do it, but you'll want to lead a group that will be able to engage and grow spiritually as they do the practice. Take your time and go slowly with this one, because it's something you have to build up to.

We've tried centering prayer in worship on a Sunday morning to introduce the concept to people, but again we didn't go twenty minutes—more like three. Otherwise it has the opposite effect it's supposed to.

The main reason I teach this corporately is to help people understand that they can use one word to draw themselves back to being still with God. The whole reason for doing centering prayer is to experience the love and presence of God.

On your own before you lead

Set a timer for twenty minutes.

Find a word or image that will draw you back to resting in God's presence.

Close your eyes, and rest in God.

Leading Centering Prayer

Say something like this as you begin to lead this practice: "Take a moment to get comfortable in your chair. Close your eyes, and take a few deep breaths. Put your phone in airplane mode, or turn it off. Phones buzzing during this exercise are very distracting."

Once everyone is still again, ask them to take a moment to think of a word or image that helps them focus on the presence of God. Then have them share their word or image with the group by saying the one word or by describing the image in a word or two. As the leader, once half or most of the people have shared their word, start the practice.

Tell them to imagine they're sitting in the presence of God, or ask them to remember how they feel when they feel close to God. As the leader, share what you imagine as you sit in the presence of God or the feeling you have when you're focused on God. If you'd like to help people further, lead a guided imagery, which I'll discuss in chapter four.

Set a timer for three minutes, and let the group know you're doing it. Tell them that when it goes off, you'll instruct them what to do. Go at least three minutes if you've already done the exercise with two minutes of silence. In a group, twenty minutes of silence is the upper end of time, and that's for the experienced only. If this is a group you lead regularly, you can increase the amount of time each time you meet.

How you end the time of silence can vary. I like to pray our way out of it. Some people use a singing bowl or chime instead of a timer. However, the less I use items and words associated with New Age spirituality, the less likely participants are to assume we're doing practices contrary to Christian teaching and tradition.

After you've prayed gently, start to debrief. Encourage people to take a moment to write down what felt significant to them as they were in the silence. By inviting people to write or draw before speaking, you allow them time to process.

After you've given the group a minute or two to write or draw, ask if anyone would like to share something that happened during the silence. Because some people will talk about *anything,* remind them that they're to talk only about what happened in the silence. You are the one who helps the whole group keep the conversation focused on how God spoke in the silence.

Let one or two people answer, and make sure you leave enough silence for other people to share. When we as leaders keep talking, people in our group think we don't want to hear what they have to say. To make sure I leave time for other people to share, I go silent. When I wonder if I've given enough time, I count slowly backward from five. By then I've quieted my anxious spirit and given enough time for people to chime in.

Then ask another question: "What was hard about this practice?" I like to ask this sooner rather than later so that the people who feel like failures know that others struggled too. This frees them up to hear from other people in the room.

Then you can continue with a few more questions, such as, "What was the best part of this practice for you?" and "Did God reveal anything to anyone during this practice?" I like to ask a few questions instead of just one, in case the one question doesn't resonate with some people.

I also do my best to keep debriefing to five minutes—or to ten when multiple people are engaging deeply. Here again, make sure you're aware of your group during the times of debrief. You may need to say, "If you've already shared, please give others a chance to share." With a larger group, I've also let people share around their table, each person having a minute to say what their experience was like.

THE ROLE OF CORPORATE SILENCE

Leading silence in a group can seem like the opposite of bringing people together to have deep spiritual conversations. However, for both the introvert and the extrovert, silence before sharing levels the playing field. Both go into the spiritual depths of their souls when given the space to go there in community. Once everyone has had time to engage deeply with God, all seem more willing to engage in the conversation, especially if you give them a few moments to write down what they processed with God during the silence.

Silence is the foundation of all the other spiritual practices in this book. Almost every chapter and practice uses silence to give space for God to speak to the hearts of those who are engaging in the practices. Therefore, if you're feeling shortchanged because this chapter has only three ways to practice silence, have no fear. There's much more to come.

If this chapter on silence scared you, remember that in the Bible, God often offered the comforting command, "Fear not." Discomfort just means you need more practice, as with anything else worth doing. If you or your group struggle with silence, go back to the two minutes of silence exercise to see if you can reset the way you're engaging with God. Find your own ideas for helping your community enter into silence together, because you know your group better than anyone else.

Now that you have three ways to lead people into silence, I pray you stand confidently as you enter into the presence of God with others. Christ quieted himself in the garden to hear the clear voice of his Father in heaven, and he invited his disciples to join him. Remember that Christ wasn't successful as he led his disciples in prayer either; they kept falling asleep. Yet he didn't stop engaging them with the Father, because he knew that was the most important piece (Matthew 26:36-46). We must teach people how to engage with the heart of God. When they don't know how to be still before the Lord, they feel alone. When they know how, they can seek what they need from him.

As you learn, consider using spiritual practices in these contexts:

- on mission trips for morning devotions
- during Sunday school to help participants focus on God
- in church as a way of being still before the Lord in worship
- in Bible studies to prepare or to meditate on the Word
- in small groups to take conversations deeper spiritually
- on retreats as a way to create some quiet space for God
- during family devotions before bed or at dinner
- before board meetings to center your heart on God's will
- at staff meetings to shift how you're thinking about the work of the church
- in planning meetings to get your focus on what God wants

Just recently, the chairperson of our church invited the board to arrive fifteen minutes early to meetings simply to sit together in silent prayer before we entered into our long, word-filled meetings. It has brought new life in Christ into the space as we start our time together on the same page: God's page.

Try not to see silence in community as limiting, but as a way to listen to God without limits.

3

EXPLORING SCRIPTURE TOGETHER

My husband and I have three dogs. They're our little family, three furry friends whose welcoming, crazy, fun presence greets everyone at the door. If you're shorter than five feet tall, you may find yourself fearing for your life. Experiencing sixty-eight pounds coming at you at eye level when you weigh only forty-eight is a lot different from being double or triple the weight and height of the dog.

When we read the Scriptures in community, we aren't the same in age, race, size, culture, gender, or socioeconomic status, so we get to hear different perspectives—if we listen. In diversity we can see the Bible from the perspective in which it was written: to all the world.

A child may notice something in the biblical narrative that gives insight to the adults in the room. Having people from different socioeconomic backgrounds opens up different ways of seeing God's economy. When we have different cultures represented, we may even see for the first time how the Scriptures weren't written in our own culture.

Scripture is always the final authority and the centerpiece of all the spiritual practices. Whatever we think we hear from God during a spiritual practice must align with Scripture, or it is not from God.

The three ways to read Scripture in this chapter can be used with young children who can't read, older adults, and every age in between. These practices are excellent as devotions on intergenerational mission trips as well as in age-specific groups. The younger the child, the more adaptations are required, but I'm always surprised how well these practices work with middle school, high school, adult, and intergenerational groups. These practices can engage the whole group in dialogue about the Scriptures, as the Word of God transforms hearts in unexpected ways.

I'll teach you about imaginative prayer, which will help you enter into lectio divina, and then lead you right into Bible art journaling. All three of these spiritual practices can be used in multiple venues. (You'll find one more Scripture-based practice in chapter seven, called Dwell in the Word.) Imaginative prayer is both the easiest of the three and the most helpful, giving us something to build on as we enter into the next practices. This is a fun spiritual practice to do with children, because they can fully engage with it right alongside adults.

IMAGINATIVE PRAYER

Imaginative prayer in its simplest form is imagining what's happening in the biblical narrative as it unfolds. This concept was created by St. Ignatius in the 1500s as a way to enter into the Scriptures and experience the presence of God.

I have always loved that the Word of God is not a dead document. Hebrews 4:12 says, "For the word of God is alive and active. Sharper than any double-edged sword, it penetrates even to dividing soul and spirit, joints and marrow; it judges the thoughts and attitudes of the heart." Reading God's Word and listening for how it can be alive in our lives through spiritual practices leads to long-term transformation of our attitudes and hearts. When we read Scripture in a different way than we usually do, we see things we missed in other traditional ways of reading and studying.

This way of seeing the Bible unfold can add a new level of reality to your life, because it's unlike other forms of study you may have used in the past. Recently a group of women, all older than fifty, told me how powerful it was to enter into the Scriptures this way. Many of them saw something they'd never seen before, even though they'd read the passage and heard it and preached it many times. Somehow imagining themselves there in the moment brought new life to the Scriptures for them.

I was first introduced to imaginative prayer when I was a young youth director in an Episcopal church. I'd never looked at the Scriptures the way we did until that day, when we were invited to imagine ourselves in the story as it was read straight from the Bible. I'll always remember that beautiful moment of entering into the Word of God. It came alive. I was fully engaged and was feeling transformed spiritually right there in the moment. When we came out of our own imaginations and remembered that we were still in a room full of people wearing modern-day clothing, that was a defining moment for me.

The person leading the exercise asked a great question: "Did anyone become someone or something in the story?" A boy of about eight said, "I became a rock along the side of the road where they were walking." This captivated me. It changed how I thought about Scripture. Having a child's perspective on Scripture is very important. I needed to see things and think about things from a younger viewpoint. As Jesus said, "Truly I tell you, anyone who will not receive the kingdom of God like a little child will never enter it" (Mark 10:15; Luke 18:17).

I had assumed I needed to be a *person* in the story as the biblical scene unfolded. But the child who put himself in the place of a rock in this scene could take in the whole story while not being responsible for anything that happened in the story. He could watch, observe, and process it all as a rock.

I felt a shift in the depths of my soul as I too became a rock along the side of the road that day. I needed to hear things in Scripture from different perspectives. God's Word was written to all the world, not just my little corner of Diana-ville. God wants us to enter into his story with our whole hearts and minds within community.

That day I became a part of God's story in a powerful way. May it be the same for you as you enter into his Word, seeing things from a different angle as you journey with others.

On your own before you lead

Find a narrative story from Scripture.
Read the passage using all your senses to imagine you are there.

Leading Imaginative Prayer

First find a passage of Scripture. Imaginative prayer works best with a narrative, so stay away from books like Psalms and Proverbs. Finding a story that covers less than twenty verses is also helpful; otherwise people can get lost in their own thoughts and distracted from the biblical story.

Second, have participants find a comfortable space where they can sit with their eyes closed and relax. They sometimes ask if they can lie down. I usually discourage this for two reasons: they may get too relaxed and fall asleep, or they may be too stimulated. However, do try different things as you use these spiritual practices. If you feel your group would get more out of lying down, try it. If that doesn't work, don't toss out the whole practice, because the failure may have been about the posture.

I believe if you set people up correctly at the beginning of a spiritual practice, almost anything can play a positive role in the outcome. I have set up a prayer room where we encouraged people to lie on a mat as they read the story of the man lying by the pool at Bethesda. My hope was that this posture would add to the experience of entering into the story instead of distracting them, and I believe it worked. We also had a baby pool of water next to the mats.

Lead your group with instructions like these:

- Take a few deep breaths. Close your eyes if that's helpful.
- Feel free to have a piece of paper in front of you with a pen so you can jot things down as you go.
- Open to the passage of Scripture in your Bible so as the story is read, you can reread something you may have missed or were surprised by.
- Imagine yourself entering into biblical times. Do whatever you can to place yourself there. You may become a person or animal in the story or an object along the way.
- Use all five of your senses to engage fully with what it would be like to be there. Notice what you see, smell, hear, touch, and taste as you're in the story. Notice sounds other

than voices. Listen for wind, water, birds, or any part of nature that may be present. What do you hear in the distance? Is there something you can taste, touch, or smell? As the story is read, become a part of it as best you can.

- Notice the facial expressions of people in the story. Notice who you are near and who you are far away from in the story. Notice who you are drawn to and who repels you. Notice tones of voice as you hear the voice not of the person reading but of the actual people in history.

As the leader, read the story slowly and carefully. When you feel you've read a part of the story for which the participants may need to spend time creating the scene, give them a moment or two before you continue reading. Stay aware of facial expressions and movements in the room. Notice if it seems like participants are straining to see something in their minds or simply trying to keep their eyes closed. The more still people are during this process, the more engaged their minds will be. Sudden movements or very slow intentional movements show they're fully entering into the story. Keep reading slowly and methodically.

If there is dialogue, read it slowly enough that participants have time to picture each person talking. Try not to add inflections to the story as you read; your inflections can alter the way people experience the story.

When appropriate, say something like this to the participants: "Stay in the story, and notice what the people in the story do next. Let this play out in your mind. Notice the emotions of the people in the story. Notice what's happening inside you at this point in the story. Try to name some of your feelings and emotions as the story wraps up."

At the end of the story, tell them to slowly open their eyes and jot down things that affected them. Ask, "What did you notice? What did you feel, hear, see, touch, or taste? What felt significant to you and to God as you witnessed the story unfold? Who were you drawn to in the story?" Feel free to add your own questions.

After you've given everyone time to jot down what they gleaned from the story, lead a discussion. I ask certain questions of myself to determine how long I let people write before we talk: How much time do we have left for this practice? What is the main goal of doing this spiritual practice today? Do I want them to grow in community or in their own personal study of the Word? And who is my audience? The younger the people in the room, the less time you need to give to writing.

Remember the halfway rule: when half the group is done writing, it's time to open it up to discussion. Sometimes it can be helpful to read the passage a second time to move deeper into the story, if you have time.

I usually ask something very general like, "Is there anything anyone would like to share with the group that happened as you became a part of the biblical story?" Almost always someone says something right away. Make sure you leave a moment of silence before you ask the next question.

Many leaders are afraid of silence and keep talking until someone tries to interrupt. Most people don't interrupt; they stay quiet until they're sure you're inviting them to speak. Try to create space so people don't need to interrupt you or anyone else. Pausing for a few seconds can create a very healthy environment for sharing.

After I ask a general question, I ask very specific questions to help those who are more concrete in their thinking, such as children younger than eighth grade. They need specific questions so they can enter into the conversation, such as . . .

▪ What did you see?

▪ What did you hear?

- What did you touch?
- What did you taste?
- What did you smell?
- Who were you in the story?
- Where did you find yourself in the story?
- Who was close to you, and who was far away?
- Whose facial expressions did you see?

Encourage participants to share in just a few sentences. If the group is small enough, encourage sharing for a minute or two. If you let them share in small groups first, ask if there were any themes they would like to share with the larger group.

Don't be afraid if people share that they had a hard time imagining or that they didn't get anything out of the process. It's good to validate that this happens. Some spiritual practices work better than others for different people. Let them know that even if they don't get anything out of this practice, they may get something out of another practice or even the same one on a different day or with a different Bible story. The Word of God is active and living, so on different days and in different stories, we hear different things from God.

Close in prayer, thanking God for the rich time of entering into his Word together.

LECTIO DIVINA, OR SACRED READING

Lectio divina is a way to meditate on and engage in God's Word. It's a monastic practice created by St. Benedict in the sixth century that became a more formal four-step process in the twelfth. It's good for us to remember that all spiritual practices were created by humans, not God, and adapted so we can go deeper in relationship with Christ. This gives us each permission to keep adapting ways to engage with the Word of God so it comes fully alive to us and to those we lead.

Normally when doing lectio divina, you read the same passage of Scripture four times slowly, pausing between each reading to reflect. The four movements of lectio divina are read, meditate, pray, and contemplate. When you're teaching lectio divina, age and time play into whether participants can do all four movements. The younger the age or the less the participants have done the practice, the fewer number of times I read the passage. The amount of time I hold the silence between each reading also hinges on these two factors.

When leading lectio divina, you can do it quickly or draw it out—from fifteen minutes to forty-five. You can choose how the group shares, how many times you read the passage, and how long you hold the silence between each time. The fifteen-minute version is great at the beginning of a meeting, and the forty-five-minute version is good to use as the main piece in a spiritual formation lesson or at a retreat. When doing the fifteen-minute version, after each reading give the whole group a moment to share about the big picture. Let three or four people share for fifteen-second bursts, and then move on. If you have forty-five minutes for this practice, pause after each reading, allow journaling for a while, and have participants share in their small groups for about five minutes each time.

I'm always surprised how fast time goes with spiritual practices, even forty-five minutes. You are the keeper of the time, so don't let it get away from you. By keeping the time and space for the group, you offer them the gift of time standing still as they meet with God. I lead a women's Bible study each week, and we usually have time for only two spiritual practices in our hour-and-a-half sessions. But sometimes I choose to do more or less in a session.

On your own before you lead

Use the same passage you'll be using with the group.

The first time you read the passage, write down a word or phrase that stands out to you.

The second time, draw or describe the image you see.

The third time, write down what it means to you today.

The fourth time, write down what God is inviting you into today.

Leading Lectio Divina

Choose a passage of Scripture that's between one and six verses long. You don't have to use a narrative story for this practice. Just about any passage will work.

When looking for a way to launch a meeting and get focused on God's agenda, find a passage that applies directly to where you think God wants the meeting to go. When talking about calling, you may use one of the passages of Scripture where Jesus calls the disciples to follow him. If you're doing devotions on a mission trip, look for passages of Scripture that mention serving. You're the leader, so it's okay to pick a passage that feels loaded in the direction you're hoping to take the meeting. After all, if you were leading a traditional devotional moment, you would make sure the passage aligned with where God wanted you all to go.

Be ready for people in your group to listen to the voice of God, not just to you. Be ready to hear what God may be saying in that moment. And be ready for God to change the direction of the meeting. Allow yourself as the leader to hear the voice of God with your group. It can be powerful when God speaks; the real test is if we'll listen. "Do not merely listen to the word, and so deceive yourselves. Do what it says" (James 1:22). This includes you.

Give people the opportunity to read the passage of Scripture you will be reading. Often I print off the passage so participants can read along as well as write on and around it. If they brought their own Bibles to the gathering, they can mark in them if they choose. At the very least, pull out Bibles so everyone can follow along.

Before you start, let the group know how many times the passage will be read. If you have at least forty-five minutes, and everyone in the room is an adult, read the passage four times. If you have less than forty-five minutes, if people in your group are younger than eighteen, or if this is the first time you've done spiritual practices with a group of adults, read the passage three times instead of four. If you have a limited amount of time or are doing the practice with children, read it twice. Before you start, think about which of the four questions you'll have them pay attention to each time it's read: What word or phrase jumped out to you? What image came to mind? What does this passage mean to you today? or, What is God inviting you to today?

After you read the passage to model reading it very slowly, ask others to read it. I encourage you to go back and forth between male and female voices, ages, and races, seeking diversity that way as well. The more diversity in any shape or form the better.

Before you read the passage the first time, ask everyone to listen for a word or phrase that stands out to them as you read. It may jump off the page at them. It may appear to be in bold as they hear it. Tell them, "Let the word or phrase pick you as I read. There is not a right or wrong answer, just the word or phrase that feels important to you today."

Encourage everyone to get in a comfortable position and to relax their minds for a moment, centering their hearts on God. Tell them, "We will pause before and after each reading to give you some personal time with Jesus." I try to wait until the room falls still and quiet for a few moments before I start. Pause for about five seconds if you have young people in your group. If you have a group of contemplative people, pause for fifteen seconds or so before you start reading.

Before you start to read, say, "Listen for a word or phrase," and then read at a very slow pace. When you finish reading the passage, pause again to let people sit with their word or phrase. You can say, "Take a moment to focus on the word or phrase that stood out to you"—that is, five seconds for under age eighteen and up to two minutes for groups used to more time sitting with God.

Speak gently, trying not to jar people from their space with God, encouraging the group to write down their word or phrase or to underline it in the Scripture passage. If you didn't provide a printout of the Scripture, have paper and pens available.

Ask them to share the word or phrase with the group—not an explanation. If they didn't notice a word or phrase, they can say, "Pass." If you're leading a large group, encourage people to quickly go around their tables and say their word or phrase. If your group is small, you can ask, "Would anyone be willing to share their word or phrase with the whole group?" If people are sitting in rows, they can share their word or phrase with someone next to them. A great way to build community is to encourage the front row to turn and face the second row, and so on, and then to pull into groups of four or five. If you move people into groups, be sure no one is left out in the process, and be sure there's no time wasted on people trying to figure out who they should share their word or phrase with.

After you give a moment to share in groups, leaving time at the end to debrief the whole exercise, say to the group, "As a different person reads the same passage of Scripture again, let an image come to mind. The image may or may not be literal; figurative images can help you process the passage and hear what God has to say. If you've done imaginative prayer before, it can be helpful, but it's not required. Not everyone has a visual mind, so if an image doesn't surface, that's okay." Remember to pause both before and after the passage is read.

Choose the next person to read the passage. Remember to consider gender, race, age, and even socioeconomic status if you can without pointing out why you are asking certain people to read. Sometimes I might ask for a male or a female, or someone who is an adult or kid, but beyond that I would not highlight much else when asking people to read. Remind participants to read slowly, letting an image come to mind as the passage is read again. After the passage has been read, give them a moment to sit with the image. If you have time, encourage people to draw the image they saw or to describe it in writing. Then ask participants to share their image with the group the same way they did their word or phrase. Encourage them not to share what they think the image means yet.

If you have a group of fifth graders or younger, stop the practice at this point. This is far enough for them. Ask a simple debrief question like, "Why do you think God pointed out this word and image to you today?"

The third time participants read the passage, tell them to listen for the meaning it has for them right then. This is less about what it means theologically and more about what it means to them as the word brushes up against their lives. Theology may inform what they're hearing, but this isn't a moment for trying to remember what they've learned about the passage in the past. Encourage them simply to consider what it means to them in the moment, as they lay this piece of Scripture over their lives.

After the Scripture passage has been read the third time, leave a little space for participants to jot down a few thoughts on paper. Then encourage the group members to process what the passage means right then in their lives. Challenge them to try to describe it to their group in a sentence or two.

Move to reading the passage for the fourth and last time. Tell the participants, "This time listen for an invitation from God. What is God inviting you to today?" Have the fourth person read the passage. Then give some space to journal for a moment and to talk with God about what he's inviting them to.

When I do this spiritual practice with junior and senior high students, I combine the third and fourth readings by saying, "As we read this passage for the third time, listen for what God may be saying to you today about this passage. What does it mean to you today, and what is God inviting you to today?"

After you've read the passage four times, have them share with their groups one last time. Let them know that there's something powerful about saying something out loud; it can make you want to commit to follow through.

Let them know if they have one minute each to share or if they have more like two to three minutes. More than three minutes for most people will feel like too much time for the group. Some people will talk ten minutes if you don't give them clear boundaries for how long to share. This way one person can't dominate the conversation, particularly if you aren't able to lead in every group. If you notice someone in a group taking more time, you can say out loud, "You should be moving to the next person if you haven't yet." This should help that person move on.

After the small-group sharing time, ask if any themes came up. Have one person per table share with the larger group. This is a great way to segue into the rest of your meeting or lesson.

Close in prayer, thanking God for being present and teaching through his Word.

Something I tried as I adapted lectio divina recently was reading a passage that was confusing yet familiar from four different Bible versions. When I first started, I wasn't sure it would work; I worried that if the word or phrase someone picked the first time the passage was read was not the same in the versions we used in the next readings, they might be confused.

I warned the group that I was trying an experiment and wasn't sure it would work, and I asked them if they were willing to try it and give me feedback. It's always a great idea to introduce something that you're trying for the first time as an experiment so the group realizes you're trying something new. This is why I like the term *practices*. We're practicing ways to engage with the living God. Sometimes when we practice, things aren't that great, but as we practice, they get better and better. We're practicing being with God.

The group loved doing lectio divina this way, as I had done it with them the original way several times before we tried the new way. They liked how it brought out deeper meaning as they read the different translations. I started with a popular version of the Bible first, the New International Version. Then I read the Amplified Bible, the New Living Translation, and finally *The Message* to give us one more angle. It was fun to listen to the participants share something new they learned about the passage as we progressed through the process. We each felt better about what God was trying to help humanity understand through the short passage we were reading. I suggest that you as a leader read all four translations of a passage and decide whether it will work with a whole group. Don't experiment; be prepared.

BIBLE ART JOURNALING

Bible art journaling is a concept that came alive for me through Shanna Noel, a pastor's wife who felt the Word of God was no longer alive and well in her life. She loved to be creative but was finding that the Word of God wasn't living and breathing life into her anymore. Something needed to change. One day she decided to start journaling in her Bible, and she felt the Word of God come alive in her again. She posted a picture on Instagram, and it went viral overnight. It has now turned into a full-time ministry, with her family on staff as well.

Shanna had no intention of transforming her idea into a company or a ministry. It was out of her time with God that she felt drawn into his heart again, fresh and new, and she wanted to pass that on to others.

This spiritual practice is tailor-made for those who like to create. They don't have to be artists; they just need to enjoy combining a love for art with the Word of God. This practice tends to work best with children, teens, and women. Children can engage with it easily because they get to draw or color instead of read. It's helpful if they can read, but that's not required when you do Bible art journaling in community. Shanna has her own way of doing Bible art journaling, and as soon as I saw the concept, I realized that doing it in combination with lectio divina gave me the structure I needed to make it come alive for me.

The first time I tried leading Bible art journaling, I led it with sixty people. First I printed out our theme verse for the weeklong conference on a half sheet of paper. I told them we were going to read the verse three times. I've learned that three is the right number because you can cover everything that most people do in Bible art journaling—write a word in the margin, draw something on the page, and journal—by the time you finish the third movement. As you lead this practice you can do one of these steps yourself after you read the passage each time. Make sure you are still paying attention to your audience so they don't check out while waiting for you to finish your art. You can always come back to your art when you are done.

The results were stunning. As participants hung their art on the wall, it was clear the images were greatly varied, even when only one verse was read. The words varied but also had something in common. God was inviting these people into relationship with him that week. It was great for me to see how spiritually deep they went when I gave them a reflective space in a crazy, spiritually busy week. It gave us a moment to pause and to see what God was doing inside these people. I led a group in Bible art journaling eight times that week, and I kept seeing God working in and through people all week. It was beautiful.

Leading Bible Art Journaling

Before anyone enters the room, put some art supplies on the center of every table. Use as many or as few art supplies as you would like; any combination works well. Consider offering colored pencils, watercolors, pens, pencils, crayons, markers, and chalk. If you know participants who have craft rooms or leftover scrapbooking supplies, invite them to bring anything they would enjoy using or sharing.

Consider the people in the group. Some will find it intimidating or distracting to see a lot of art supplies on the table, and some will get more excited the more variety you provide. Sometimes I don't put crayons on a table for middle school students, because some of them will assume I'm treating them like little kids. However, putting crayons out for adults gives them permission to be artistic and creative like a little kid. If you have a very diverse group, lean toward colored pencils, which seem to appeal to both children and adults. If you know the group will be nervous about not being skilled enough to do art, remember that less is more; be very specific as you instruct them.

Print out the passage of Scripture you'd like the group to process together. Do this on any size of paper as long as you leave large margins on one side of the Scripture. I print using the landscape orientation with two columns of text, leaving a generous margin on one side of the verse. I then print out and cut the page in half to create two identical pages. The best passage length for this practice is one to six verses. The younger the age, the fewer verses you should use.

As you read aloud the passage of Scripture the first time, encourage the group to listen for a word or phrase. Have them write it big in the margin. If you have a nonartistic group, encourage them to use a specific art supply, like a black marker.

When the next person reads the passage, instruct the participants to see if God reveals an image to them that they can draw in the margin with the words or over the words. Tell them that as the passage is read, they can feel free to start drawing to create what God is showing them. If you're working with fifth-grade children and younger, this is where you can stop the practice and debrief with them.

The third and last time you read the passage, have them listen all the way through and then journal—over their image or in the margin—what God is teaching them through the passage, what it means to them today, and what God is inviting them to do.

I used this process with a group of people from our church to create fifteen different canvases for a sermon series on the Psalms of Ascent. Not everyone chose to create artwork through the process of lectio divina. But when I walked them through it with the psalm they had chosen, they were all able to create an amazing piece of art that depicted their psalm. Some painted and others collaged their images. Some used large letters over the image, and others painted words across the image. For fifteen Sundays in a row, it was beautiful to have someone different stand up and share about his or her piece of art while it stood on an easel. The artwork was then put on the wall for the rest of the series.

READING SCRIPTURE CORPORATELY

When we do Scripture-based spiritual practices together, we learn more than if we're reading the Word alone. The original reading of the Word of God was cooperative. No one had his or her own copy of the Scriptures. When we read them together, we go deeper in Christ and deeper spiritually together.

Consider using one of these places where corporate reading can happen:

- on mission trips
- at vacation Bible school
- during Sunday school with any age
- in church
- in Bible studies
- in small group settings
- on retreats
- for family devotions
- during board meetings
- in staff meetings
- in prayer rooms
- in planning meetings

Sometimes you'll worry that someone isn't creative enough or won't engage in spiritual practices. Consider giving this person the gift of thinking differently about Scripture. These practices and God have the ability to awaken the right side of the brain even in very left-brained people.

There are many spiritual practices in this book, all of which should be grounded in the Word of God. Engaging with the Scriptures is extremely important when you're leading a group that's nervous about spiritual practices being too mystical or New Age. Using the Word of God during all spiritual practices gives anxious believers the grounding they need to enter deeply into relationship with God through spiritual practices.

4

SIMPLE PRAYERS *that* TRANSFORM COMMUNITY

Eᴀʀʟʏ ɪɴ ᴍʏ ᴍɪɴɪsᴛʀʏ ᴠᴏᴄᴀᴛɪᴏɴ, when I first started leading others, I developed an extreme fear of flying. Since I was leading overseas mission trips regularly, this was a very real problem. I was supposed to be the one who was the calmest and most put together.

I couldn't fly without my heart racing at takeoff and landing. My hands clutched either the armrest or the arm of the person next to me. I wasn't okay. Though I knew I couldn't give up my calling, I could barely manage myself, let alone manage a whole group. I also didn't have the ability to ask God for comfort in those moments. I needed a way to connect with God but didn't know how I was going to do it.

Then an idea came to me: I needed to picture God holding the plane in his hand. A sense of peace came over me right away. I needed to remember that God was in charge, not me. God was responsible for our lives, not me. In my mind, his strong, firm, yet gentle hand went under the belly of the plane.

Then turbulence started. My body tightened again. So I imagined God's hands flicking the demons off the plane one by one. I've used this visual prayer for more than fifteen years now, and it has rewired my brain. I no longer fear flying. My heart no longer races. I no longer clutch the armrest. I simply trust that I am literally in God's hands.

This chapter gives three very simple ways to pray in our high-anxiety, overly busy world. They can help stressed-out people pause even for a minute to experience the healing power of God. These three ways to pray, when used regularly, have the power to transform the mind and soul both in the moment and long term.

You may not have an issue with flying, but most of us battle something. If you aren't someone who regularly struggles with anxiety, remember a time you had an anxious moment. Let yourself feel it for a moment. Now picture the opposite happening. Instead of picturing the worst thing that could happen, picture how God himself can intervene and take things in the direction he wants them to go. Picture the outcome you need, not the outcome you fear. See healing occurring. See the plane not crashing. See God overcoming what scares you the most. Picture God doing something to correct the situation. Once you have this prayer image, you can use it any time you feel anxiety rise up in you.

When we have intense anxiety, it's very difficult to pray, so find your image prayer before you're in the situation again. A friend of mine and former missionary in Austria used image prayer while battling cancer. As she sat for hours receiving chemotherapy, she practiced watching PAC-MAN chomp up all the cancer cells in her body. In her blog, *Tandem Living*, she encouraged readers to pray that prayer with her. She is now in remission and has written a book called *Tandem Living* that includes several image prayers she uses.

SIMPLE PRAYER

One simple prayer in Scripture is the Lord's Prayer. It's simple enough to memorize, and it can come to mind easily, even in stressful situations. People recite the Lord's Prayer in the midst of near-death experiences when stress is very high as well as when they're at the end of their life and can't remember much else.

Some of the psalms are simple prayers, easily used as responsive readings to pray together. In other psalms, groups of words are repeated multiple times. Repeating them comforts our souls with the truth of God's attributes. When we repeat phrases, they're more likely to be remembered and then retrieved when needed most. Psalm 136 is a great example of this, as the phrase "his love endures forever" is repeated for twenty-six verses.

When even simple prayers fail us, the Holy Spirit intercedes for us when we're without words: "The Spirit helps us in our weakness. We do not know what we ought to pray for, but the Spirit himself intercedes for us through wordless groans. And he who searches our hearts knows the mind of the Spirit, because the Spirit intercedes for God's people in accordance with the will of God" (Romans 8:26-27).

When we're too anxious to pray, the Holy Spirit intercedes as we picture our prayers for what we need. Scripture tells us exactly how to address anxiety:

> Do not be anxious about anything, but in every situation, by prayer and petition, with thanksgiving, present your requests to God. And the peace of God, which transcends

all understanding, will guard your hearts and your minds in Christ Jesus.

Finally, brothers and sisters, whatever is true, whatever is noble, whatever is right, whatever is pure, whatever is lovely, whatever is admirable—if anything is excellent or praiseworthy—think about such things. Whatever you have learned or received or heard from me, or seen in me—put it into practice. And the God of peace will be with you. (Philippians 4:6-9)

God gave us the gift of anxiety to help us take care of ourselves and others when something bad is happening. As Paul said above directly, we are to address everything through prayer.

On your own before you lead

Think of an anxiety-producing event in your life. Pause. See if you can find an image that helps you pray through the anxiety.

Leading Simple Prayer

Ask the group to think of something that makes them anxious to the point of having no ability to think straight. For high-anxiety people, it's best to start with something that produces only a small amount of anxiety. Later they can work up to a more anxiety-provoking thought.

If you're willing, give the group an example from your own life. You're also welcome to use some of my examples if your anxieties are too personal or too overwhelming to share with a group. Note that after you've led this practice, it's a good idea to find some quality space for yourself to address what's going on inside you.

When you use examples, it does a variety of things for the group. First, they feel less crazy themselves for having anxieties; they're reminded that everyone has them. It also gives them permission to enter into the practice at a deep level.

If participants are willing, have them share their anxieties around their table, or have people name a few anxieties in the large group. This can help them know they aren't alone in the hard place of anxiety. It can also help low-anxiety people brainstorm ideas for when they actually do feel anxious.

Ask the group to think of something minor that makes them anxious. Then ask where they feel it in their body. Most people feel it in a particular place. They may have sweaty palms or a rapid heart rate. Some get butterflies in their stomach or heaviness in their chest. Encourage them to picture the opposite—or what they need to be at peace and have no physical symptoms.

Then ask them to picture God taking control of the situation. For example, if a participant has a recurring nightmare, he can picture the way God may intervene in the midst of the dream. I used to have recurring nightmares that I was on stage and I didn't know my lines. These nightmares came when I wasn't feeling prepared. So when I slept and that nightmare happened, I had someone in my dream hand me a script. The nightmares have stopped completely. And I don't feel as much anxiety in my awake moments either.

Encourage participants to ask God to show them how he wants to change anxiety-creating images so they can come to a place of less anxiety. Have them imagine how God may take care of the anxiety-inducing situation. Encourage the group to close their eyes and focus on a new positive image of God's intervention in the anxiety. Give them a few minutes in silence to sit with their image. Make sure you tell them how long (at least a minute, but not much more than five, depending on your group). You could even ask the group how much time they'd like, to give you an idea of what they're up for.

As the time of silence is closing, encourage them to ask God if he wants to show them one last thing before they exit the image prayer. Pause for a few moments. Gently encourage them to wiggle their toes and fingers and then to find themselves back in the room.

After you've welcomed the group back, take a moment to let them jot down something they don't want to forget from the experience. This helps introverts share with the group when it's time. For extroverts, it's a way to remember long term and to be concise when they share with the group.

After everyone has written something down, encourage them to share something significant that happened during the silence. Have them do this in smaller groups or with the whole group, depending on what you're trying to accomplish. For example, you may want small groups getting to know each other at a deeper level, or you may want to unite a large group by having large-group sharing. Or have them share one-on-one. Ask them what they liked best about the practice or what was most helpful. Then ask them what was hard about the practice.

Troubleshooting can also be a part of the debriefing process. If someone's prayer image resulted in distress or discomfort, it's important to respond. In one session, a woman told us that her image prayer was of her deceased loved one alive again, but when she came out of prayer, she was hit with the reality that he wasn't alive. That distressed her, raising her anxiety level instead of granting the peace Christ had to offer in her time of need.

As the leader, help people like her manage negative experiences by encouraging them to find different images. In this case, I asked the woman, "What would it be like to picture your loved one in the presence of God instead?" Then she had the space to see if that would be a helpful image prayer or not.

As the leader, keep troubleshooting at the forefront of your mind. There will be moments when the spiritual practice doesn't produce any fruit. That's okay. However, a sense of failure when doing a spiritual practice or a disturbing thought could become a troubling long-term issue for someone. You don't want people leaving the space feeling that they can't pray or can't hear from God. Address these issues gently in the moment, if at all possible. People who haven't shared publicly may be reassured as well.

If a person's anxiety or other issue seems to be too deep or complicated, offer more help at the end of the session. As always when dealing with potential mental health issues, refer that person to a professional rather than attempting to provide solutions yourself.

This is why quality time for group debriefing after each spiritual practice is essential. It's also the main time people connect with each other spiritually during the practice. Always remind the group that no one is giving professional advice, and all need to refrain from trying to fix each other.

GUIDED IMAGERY

Guided imagery is another form of image prayer that often helps people struggling with worry. One of my favorites is encouraging the group to picture Jesus sitting on the throne with a box at his feet to put worries into. The first time I used this with a youth group, one of the high school guys said to me, "You are my favorite youth pastor." But his compliment wasn't really about me. He had experienced the presence of the living God in his real-life anxieties, and God was transforming his soul. When I lead this practice, I often say, "If things are coming back out of the box, ask Jesus to put them back in and put his foot on the lid." This usually provokes a few knowing chuckles.

Leading Guided Imagery

Start with asking the group to sit comfortably in their chairs and close their eyes. For some people, closing their eyes is scary because they think things like, *What if no one else closes their eyes, and I look silly?* or, *What if I fall asleep?* I repeat, "Close your eyes," several times until most have their eyes closed. I often add, "This spiritual practice doesn't usually work with eyes open. If you think you'll fall asleep, find something you can stare at that will still let you use your imagination."

Encourage the group to relax and take a few deep breaths. After a few moments, tell them you're going to describe a scene with Jesus in it. Add something like, "If the scene isn't working for you, adjust it to be what you need it to be. Let my voice fade away as you find yourself in the presence of God."

As you start to describe the scene, talk slowly and deliberately so participants create the scene in their minds as you talk. Ask them to picture Jesus Christ sitting on the throne. Encourage them to notice the details of the throne, and Jesus. Try not to explain much. Let them make the image what they need it to be.

Then say, "Now imagine a box at the feet of Jesus that you can put all your worries and anxieties into." Don't describe the box or say what anxieties or worries to place in it. Give them time to picture it. Say things like, "Watch your cares and anxieties go into the box" and "Take time to see which worries try to come back out of the box. Have Jesus himself grab the items and put them back in, and maybe even put his foot back on the lid of the box."

During debriefing, people seem to enjoy telling others about what their box looked like and why. Some describe it as looking very ornate or as very plain. One person said the box started out large, and as Jesus took care of the stress and anxieties, it became smaller and smaller.

After you feel the group has had some quality time with Jesus handling their cares, worries, and anxieties, encourage them to see if Jesus has anything to say to them before they end the time of prayer.

Then encourage them to wiggle their toes and fingers and to let their eyes flutter open and notice they're in a room with other people again.

Consider having them draw or write down something they saw or felt was significant as they were in prayer during this time. After you've given them time to process on paper, encourage them to share what happened during their time with Jesus and the box.

After they've shared with the group, let them know this is a prayer they can use when worries are racing when they're trying to fall asleep or as they quiet themselves before they do a large task.

As the leader, you can create different guided imagery using Scripture as your guide. For example, use Revelation 3:20: "Here I am! I stand at the door and knock. If anyone hears my voice and opens the door, I will come in and eat with that person, and they with me." Or paint a picture for a group of people who may or may not be believers to give them an opportunity to interact with Jesus knocking at their heart's door.

Another image is that of Jesus interacting with children. "Jesus said, 'Let the little children come to me, and do not hinder them, for the kingdom of heaven belongs to such as these'" (Matthew 19:14). I've heard mixed reviews on this. For some who've experienced trauma in childhood, having Jesus interact with them as a child has brought deep emotional healing. But

I've had a few women tell me that they didn't like the idea of being children again with the male figure being the adult.

As you lead guided imagery, be aware that each person is bringing his or her full self to the imagery and entering in. The more you can gently guide, the more participants will be able to create scenes in their heads themselves. For example, with Jesus interacting with the children, let them decide if they become a child in the scene or if they are their current age.

During the debriefing, you get to hear what worked and what didn't work in the imagery. Some people aren't as visual as others, so this process can be difficult for them, but that doesn't mean they shouldn't try it. It could be a way of waking up the other side of their brain.

WORD FOR THE YEAR

Back in 2004, I was first introduced to Word for the Year by a close friend of mine. Each New Year's Eve, their small group of friends would come to their party with a word they hoped would help shape their spiritual walk that year. Before midnight, they all sat around the dinner table and discussed the word they had chosen the year before and how it had shaped and transformed them. Then they revealed their word for the new year to the group and shared how they hoped God would shape them. We each also chose a passage of Scripture that helped explain or support the word for the year.

One person took notes, because almost always someone forgot their word. It was also nice to have notes to look back on. That person then printed it out with a group picture and sent a copy to the whole group so we could be praying for each other all year. At the end of the time of sharing, before midnight, we took time to pray for one another, asking God to use our words to transform us into the people God was calling us to be.

The Word for the Year lets a single word guide you throughout the year. This one word should describe how you believe God wants to transform you. For example, one year my husband felt God was asking him to be more patient, so his word for the year became *patience*. Another year he felt God calling him to be more creative, so *create* became his word for the year.

Each word becomes a very simple way to pray your way through your year at any given moment. It can guide you like a rudder on a boat. It can be something you're asking for your life or a way you'd like to see God guide and direct you throughout the year.

Sometimes the word can sustain you through difficult years. I've experienced three years when a one-word prayer sustained me. It was comforting to know God knew the words I needed even before anything had occurred. These words carried me in ways I hadn't expected at the beginning of each year. The year I picked *health*, both my husband and my father had near-death medical issues, and my sister's house caught on fire, displacing seven—and sort of eight, as they had started an adoption process that was jeopardized due to the fire.

I had chosen *health* to commit to being healthy that year. I hadn't picked it for anyone but myself. As I sat in the middle of that year, feeling helpless and anxious, I gently reminded myself that God himself had given me my word for the year. He was in charge of the health of all the people in my family. He was near when I was feeling overwhelmed. That year my word wasn't just about my own health like I thought it was but also about the health of loved ones.

You can lead this practice in ways that increase its community effects. Encouraging people to come prepared with their word for the year before they arrive gives them space to find their word and share it with the group. At our church, we talk about Word for the Year during one of the first worship services of the new year, and then we give people a week to listen for the voice of God. The next week, during worship, we hand our words in in written form. We don't verbally share our words with one another, but our senior pastor types them up so we can see one another's words and pray for each other. Throughout the year, people share their words here and there to remind others to be praying.

Another way to lead this practice is to take some time together to listen for the voice of God. Few people take time to be still or be silent on their own, so offer them the gift of a few moments of silence in a large-group setting. One year I led two hundred leaders in a moment of silence to see if God would give each of us our word for the year. I had the strong sense that God wanted to do a mighty work through a very short time of silence that had been allotted during a worship service. However, I could feel the tension rise in the room as I led the practice. I can still feel the coldness and confusion coming from the group as I started to lead.

I prayed silently, *God, I trust you. I know you want to speak to your people. Help us listen and hear the word you have for each of us in this room.* As we came out of that silence, I took a deep breath and asked if anyone wanted to share the word God had given them. Suddenly the words were flowing from the group. It was like water to my soul. God spoke; they listened.

One year later, at that same ministry leadership gathering, I was standing in line at Starbucks, and someone approached me and said, "I want to thank you for leading us in the Word for the Year spiritual practice last year."

I was stunned and shyly said, "You're welcome. My pleasure. It's fun for me. Thanks for letting me lead."

"I don't think you understand," he replied. "I thought all this spiritual direction was a bunch of New Age stuff, and when you led that Word for the Year thing last year, I was really skeptical, yet intrigued—so intrigued that I started going to a spiritual director just to see what it was all about. It took me six months to hear my word for the year, but today, as I stand before you, I'm a different man. You can ask my wife. She's right here." I turned and met a lovely woman who simply nodded and smiled as goosebumps went up and down my arms and tears welled in my eyes.

One word. Two leaders standing in obedience. Lives changed and transformed. When a spouse and a leader is transformed by God, many others have the chance to be transformed as well.

Leading Word for the Year

Before you start leading this practice, take a moment to share your word for the year from the year before. Share how it shaped you and transformed you. If this is the first time you've heard of this concept, share the word you've picked for this year and how you hope God will use it to lead and guide you. Try to share personally about how the Word for the Year concept has impacted you or how you hope it will.

Keep it brief, but share a bit of your own experience so they can understand the concept. Feel free to read my examples out loud, but your own story would be better. Be real, be genuine, be authentic. That's how spiritual practices have transformative power in your life as well as in the lives of others.

Let the group know you're going to keep a very specific amount of time of silence so they can settle into the time and space appropriately. Depending on the group size and abilities, this exercise can take anywhere from one minute to fifteen minutes—or even thirty minutes if you encourage them to go outside, walk, journal, or create something artistically that depicts God's leading. It depends on how you ask people to listen.

Remember that there may be someone in the room who isn't familiar with listening prayer. Some have never sat and listened for God to speak; they may have always done the talking. When I remember this and assess my group, I make sure I'm saying things that help those people participate. If they don't participate, it can distract the whole group.

Encourage the group to get comfortable in their chairs and to take a few deep breaths to relax. Ask them to become aware of the presence of God. If they've done some of the other spiritual practices in this chapter, encourage them to find a similar way of engaging with God.

Let them know that after you pray, you'll set your timer for a few minutes so everyone can sit in silence together and listen for the word God is giving them for the year. Remind them in that moment that you're setting the timer for X number of minutes after you pray. Then pray a simple prayer, asking the Holy Spirit to come and meet with each person in the room individually. Don't pray more than a sentence or two.

Then stop talking! It's far too easy to keep talking. This may be because we don't trust God will speak. Out of fear, we fill the silence. Some of us presume we know what God wants to say to our group, so we say it just in case they don't listen for the voice of God. You need to trust God with these moments. The first few times I did this, I held my breath, internally freaking out that nothing was going to happen.

As you're quiet and sitting with God, you too can focus on your word for the year. You can be listening for your own word, or you can pray that those in the room would be able to hear their word.

Some leaders feel that they must enter into the practice at the same time as the group for it to be effective, but I try to do my individual work before I enter into this time with others.

That way I can be fully present to others and allow the work that the Spirit is doing in the room. Also, my responsibility to watch the time distracts me as I try to meet with God. And I often find myself having strong emotions as I listen for the voice of God, so it's hard to switch gears from my time with God to being a good leader for others. Finally, if I do the practice with the group, I miss the cues that I talked about in chapter one, such as body language and the feel of the room. Figure out what works best for you.

Once you've held the silence for the amount of time you stated at the beginning, gently pray a prayer of thanksgiving for the Holy Spirit being present. If it was a long time of silence, encourage the group to wiggle their toes and fingers to bring them back into the room or to awaken them from a little nap.

Debrief depending on how much time you have. Ask participants to share their word with the whole group, or have them turn to someone near them and discuss what their word means to them. I highly recommend having them write their word down somewhere in a place where others can see it or just themselves.

Be sure to add that they can still be in process of listening for their word for the year. They can enter into discussion with others by saying words they're considering or by talking about a concept, if they don't have a specific word yet. Sometimes discussing out loud is a part of discovering their word.

BREATH PRAYER

Breath prayer is a very simple two-phrase prayer that's prayed as you breathe in and out. It is especially helpful for people experiencing deep anxiety. I've taught it to people who have a difficult time falling asleep at night due to racing thoughts and to people who wake up in the middle of the night with racing thoughts. You can create the prayer personally or use an existing one that fits well for you. One ancient and popular breath prayer is the Jesus Prayer: "Lord Jesus Christ, Son of God, have mercy on me, a sinner." I use these words regularly as anxiety rises in my soul, letting them wash over me, reminding me that Jesus is on the throne, and he is in control. Once I have the words, I can start breathing deeply and come to a place of calm in my soul.

When our emotions are high, our brains are flooded with stress hormones that restrict our ability to think clearly or positively, or to relax. Breathing slowly and deeply resets our nervous system and can literally help us to think straight. Recently I encouraged someone who was trying to work but was too overwhelmed to pause and breathe her breath prayer at work. Once the inner self is calm, we can ask God, *Why am I experiencing so much stress?* Once we know the source of the stress, we can create a more specific breath prayer, if desired.

One of the biggest stressors for leaders is feeling we aren't leading well. As a leader, create a general breath prayer that may go something like this: "Lord Jesus Christ, thank you that you are God, and I am not." If we leaders could breathe this prayer more often, we would probably find ourselves being better leaders.

One of my in-the-moment breath prayers I use when leading is, "Jesus, remind me I'm not a doctor. Amen." All too often I'm deluded into considering myself a doctor being called to a life-and-death situation, and the faster I get there, the better the outcome will be. I've learned over the years that I must trust God to be the one who has me arrive on the scene at the right moment in a person's life. It's easy to lose sight of the fact that God has been working on people before I entered the picture.

It's okay for some phone calls to go to voicemail. Voicemails can be listened to after finishing what you're doing. Some text messages requesting your immediate response can wait until the next morning. Just because someone says jump, you don't have to respond with, "How fast and how high?" A breath prayer can actually offer you the space to think through what must be addressed right now and what can wait. As you breathe in and out, let the words of your prayer speak to your heart and mind so God can do the work in you and others that he needs to do.

I've also used breath prayer in yoga class. When I first started yoga, I listened for the things people had warned me about regarding it. I was exhausted trying to make sure the instructor wasn't brainwashing me spiritually, as all I was trying to do was make my back feel better. When the yoga instructor said, "Find your intention" and "Find your breath," I settled into a breath prayer that grounded me in Christ for the class. I left class feeling that Jesus and I had just had a really good workout. It became a fun way to go deeper in my relationship with Christ instead of worrying about going far afield in my spiritual life. At our church, we have led exercise classes with a focus on moving our bodies as we worship Christ. (More about that in chapter six: "Active Prayer with One Another.")

One way I bring breath prayer alive in a prayer room is by providing sculpting clay. First, participants work the clay as they're creating their own breath prayer or as they sit and calmly breathe their prayer over and over again. As I'm working the clay and praying for God to speak, I often create something unexpected. This gives me a window into what God may be saying to me at that moment.

Our children and teens have more sensory and focus issues than we've ever known before. One of the ways we can combat these issues is to give them something to manipulate with their hands. The clay can become a way for them to hear the voice of God; for most, it isn't a distraction, as we may have thought in the past.

Leading Breath Prayer

Lead the participants by saying something like this: "Take a moment to find your own breath prayer. Think of a name for God that has meaning for you. Say that name in your mind as you breathe in. As you exhale, ask God to give you what you need from him or what you need to give up to him. Pray that prayer silently as you breathe out." Focus on the words as you breathe in and out for a minute or two before you lead this practice.

Have participants share their breath prayer with the group as well as how they created it and how it has served them in the last few moments that they've been breathing and praying it.

Ask them to think of the name for God that impacts them. Encourage them to breathe in deeply as they think of this name. Encourage them to breathe out a few short phrases that express what they need from God or need to give to God. Also encourage them to focus on their breathing. Once they have a good breathing pattern, invite them to begin to pray their breath prayer silently, aligning it with their breathing.

Let them know how long you're going to give them to breathe in and out so they can engage with this breath prayer well.

When the time expires, have them slowly say their breath prayer out loud and then say amen.

Debrief by asking the group if they'd like to share their breath prayer and why it has meaning for them.

PRAY

When I was a kid, I was introduced to an acronym to help me know how to pray: ACTS, which stands for adoration, confession, thanksgiving, and supplication. I had no idea what *adoration* was, *confession* was also a tough word, and *thanksgiving* I understood. But then came the word *supplication*, which always seemed too hard to understand. When I became a youth director, I decided I needed an acronym that students could readily use and understand. One day, as I was writing up a lesson plan, the acronym PRAY suddenly became way too easy a solution. It was exactly what I was looking for for my students. It went like this:

- Praise and give thanks
- Repent
- Ask
- Yield

I was excited that God would be so gentle and kind to give me exactly what I needed, and I realized he wanted to give this to my students as well.

Praise and give thanks. I clarify the difference between praise and thanksgiving this way: praise is declaring who God is, and thanking God is sharing what he has done. With large groups, I introduce this part of prayer before we sing a song. While we sing, I invite them to walk forward and write words of praise on a large wipe board or large sheet of paper. Sometimes we have two stations: one for writing words of praise and the other for writing ways participants can thank God for what he has done in their lives.

When I lead this in a time of journaling, I encourage people to write words and praise in their journals. If they get stuck after one word, I tell them to write that word down on the page and try to think of a word of praise for each letter of that word.

Repent. To repent is to ask for forgiveness. Leading this part can give you the opportunity to share the gospel of Jesus Christ, especially if you're teaching a group of people who may not all know him as Lord and Savior. Or simply lead a group that wishes to remember the gift of forgiveness that only Christ can give. Engage participants in taking time to ask God for

forgiveness; the significant piece is experiencing his forgiveness. I like to create ways people can name their sin and
then take opportunities to watch the sin disappear.

One time I was on a quiet beach with about twelve high
school students. We had decided that we wanted to spend some
time connecting with God, so we each took a stick and spread
out far enough apart so we could freely write or draw our con-
fessions to God in the wet sand. As the waves came and washed
away those words and images, we watched our sins disappear
before our very eyes. As I watched my writing dissolve in the
sand, tears came, and I heard God whisper, "It is done. It is
gone. I have taken this sin from you at the cross." Yet one letter
remained: T, which was like a cross. I was awestruck that Jesus
had given me such a physical visual, as if he himself had come
down and written in the sand right in front. I felt known in my
sin—and deeply forgiven in my sin as well.

I've also led a group of women in writing a letter, asking
for forgiveness, then sending their letter through the shredder
so they could experience what it's like to have their sin de-
stroyed. I've also led students in writing their sins on small
pieces of wood or paper and throwing them into a fire, never
to be seen again.

Very early in my ministry, two girls expressed great sorrow
over their sexual sins and said they couldn't forgive themselves.
We walked down to a lake, gathering a few rocks as we went.
When we got to the lake, I encouraged them to (silently) name
specific ways they felt they had sinned against God and their
own bodies. Then I said, "When you're ready, throw those rocks
as far as you can into the lake." As they threw the rocks, they
became giddy with the joy, knowing they were fully forgiven
and didn't have to return to this sin and guilt. They both were
crying and smiling as they turned back toward me.

As the psalmist wrote, "As far as the east is from the west, so far has he removed our transgressions from us" (Psalm 103:12). Moments like these remind me what an honor and privilege it is to watch God transform souls. Spiritual practices are also one of the best ways for people to experience God with others.

Ask. Ask God for what you need, and ask him to meet others' needs. Use the anti-anxiety prayers you just learned from this book. Throughout the rest of the book, you'll learn other ways to ask God for things—prayer walks, prayers for discernment, and more.

I recently did a four-day retreat with one hundred people from nine churches. We set up a prayer room, and each group signed up for a forty-five-minute slot. At one of the stations, we had a prayer wall with a huge piece of paper on which people could write prayer requests. After writing, they were invited to pray for others' requests there. They were then asked to trace their hand over the request. It was powerful for participants not only to see that their request had been prayed for but also to lay their hands over someone else's request as they prayed.

Yield. To yield is to pause and listen for the voice of God. Take moments to yield so you can share with the group how you enjoy yielding to and listening to God. Personal stories of how you've met with God can help your group understand and dig in deeper. For example, use the practice in chapter two, My Thoughts Versus God's Thoughts, and then lead right into Palms Up, Palms Down.

Once you've introduced the idea of yielding once or twice, and you and your team have found it effective, take time as a group to name different ways you can yield to God together.

This PRAY outline could be used to lead a prayer session with a group on a regular basis, just switching up the ways you lead each letter. Use the brainstorming session as a way to debrief together. This will help participants think about ways they can do it on their own at home.

The PRAY practice can help people pray daily using different ways to connect with God. For example, each day they could take two minutes on each letter and have a quality eight minutes with God, covering all the bases. Or they could lengthen each letter and spend twenty minutes to an hour meeting with the living God.

Consider using these practices . . .

- on mission trips, when you want to ask God what he wants the group to do
- at vacation Bible school (kids can imagine Jesus interacting with them)
- during Sunday school, as a way to hear from God directly
- in church, to offer a different way to be present with God
- in Bible studies, to be more aware what the Word of God is doing in our souls
- in small groups, for deeper discussions about what God is doing in their hearts
- on retreats, as a way to relax in God's presence
- as family devotions at dinner or before bed

PROCESSING LIFE TOGETHER

FOR THE PAST TWENTY-FIVE YEARS, I've been journaling regularly. In *Childhood Disrupted*, author Donna Jackson Nakazawa wrote that journaling for twenty minutes a day can actually provide physical healing. For me, journaling was a tangible way to feel more connected to God.

When I left home for college, I wanted to grow in my faith, and I was looking for practical ways to do it. I'd learned during my high school years that good Christians do daily devotions. I knew I wanted to do them too, but I wasn't sure how I'd do them in a way meaningful for me or how I'd make time each day.

During my freshman year, my English professor required journaling every day for her class. I was sure it was a punishment rather than a way to learn and grow. I was a horrible speller, so I hated to write. And I concluded it might be the worst assignment I would ever experience. I also thought I'd pull one over on my professor and turn my journaling time into a conversation with God; that way I would at least grow spiritually.

That professor can now say, "The joke's on you." Through her prompting, I learned and grew in both my writing skills and my spiritual formation because of her journaling assignment. It grew me emotionally, spiritually, and relationally more than anything else. When that semester was over, I continued writing in my journal through the next semester, the summer, and the next semester.

And then it happened. I can still feel that moment in my dorm room during my sophomore year of college. A betrayal by my two closest guy friends broke my heart. My world had collapsed all around me. I ran to my journal to work it out.

I found myself looking back page after page, months and years, trying to uncover where it had all come undone. How could I not have seen what was going on right in front of my face? I was stunned. I was hurt and broken in a way I couldn't share with my peers. I kept trying to find in my journal what I'd missed. And there, in my own handwriting, was the presence of God—not the reasons why friends had betrayed me but the love of Christ as I walked in darkness.

I hadn't noticed God whispering through the words I was writing, God speaking through the Scriptures I hadn't heard, though I had written them in my journal. He was there even when I couldn't see him. I never would have known the nearness of God had I not documented it all along the way.

In my attempt to try to do devotions, God had honored my heart's cry. He was near. I hadn't known what to do or how to do it; I'd just started talking to God in my journal. Then I'd written one Bible verse a day in my journal.

It was beautiful to see how he had been walking with me daily as my story was unfolding, though I didn't notice his presence or even his need to be present in my life at that time. This realization transformed me in an instant. God was pursuing me when I thought I was pursuing him. Keep this in mind as you do spiritual practices for yourself and with others.

One of the best ways to allow God to do a transforming work in our souls is to let him enter into our thoughts. Inviting God into what he already sees can be a large part of our healing process. When we bring our real life to God—the good, the bad, and the ugly—he can work on us.

Using the four spiritual practices in this chapter, we can get as real as we're willing to get with God, who already knows it all. When we strip away our false selves and lay ourselves before the living God, that's when God can do his best work.

THE BIBLICAL AND SPIRITUAL PERSPECTIVE ON PROCESSING OUR LIVES

You have searched me, LORD,
    and you know me.
You know when I sit and when I rise;
    you perceive my thoughts from afar.
You discern my going out and my lying down;
    you are familiar with all my ways. . . .
Search me, God, and know my heart;
    test me and know my anxious thoughts.
See if there is any offensive way in me,
    and lead me in the way everlasting.
        (Psalm 139:1-3, 23-24)

God already knows what we're thinking and feeling. We can't hide anything from him in our lives, hearts, or minds. For some, this can feel overwhelming as they experience their internal dialogue as too awful or unrighteous for God to handle or accept. In a way, this is correct. God is holy, and he can't be in the presence of sin. Therefore, we need Jesus Christ to cover our sin with his blood so we can boldly stand before God without sin. It's actually a good thing that people think their internal lives are too dirty for God because they find themselves needing Christ desperately.

JOURNALING

It may feel counterproductive to journal in a room with lots of people. Yet journaling with others is very powerful. There's something about someone else holding the silence for you and helping you stay focused on something specific that can take you deeper than when journaling on your own.

Recently I was leading a journaling session with a group of young adult singles. It ended up being one of the richest nights of conversation they'd ever had as a group, because they journaled before they were led in a corporate discussion on what God was doing in their lives. I gave them a prompt to journal as if talking to God as their spouse and then held the silence in the room for them for just a few minutes. I then encouraged them to share with people at their table what they'd gotten out of their time with God.

Journaling works well because it gives introverts time to process what they're thinking and write it down. It helps extroverts narrow down what they're thinking into something more concise, so they don't dominate the conversation. In addition, most people who say they'd never journal realize it can be helpful and productive.

Journaling works well after a speaker, as an aid in small-group discussions, and if a lot of information is given in a meeting. Journaling after moments like those gives space to everyone in the room to process what God is doing.

If you think the word *journaling* will turn off people in your group, call it free writing. Speak in simple terms as you explain things. Say something like, "Take a few minutes to write down a few thoughts about what you just heard. Feel free to talk to God and let him know how you feel about this topic, or write out what God is doing in your life in this moment."

If you provide paper and pens, point out that those are for participants' use. If you know you're going to do this practice before an event, and you will be communicating with the group, invite them to bring their own journal. As someone who journals regularly, I would much rather use my ongoing journal than start a new one or write on a separate piece of paper. God has spoken to me clearly in the past through journaling, and if it's not in my journal, it becomes clutter instead of a profound piece of my story. Also, if a journal isn't in chronological order, it's hard to locate past writings.

Tell participants that there will be a moment when they can share what they wrote about, but they won't be required to read anything or share anything they don't want to. Whatever they write is between them and God.

After you've held the silence for three to thirty minutes, depending on your audience and how much time you have. Draw everyone back together with a one-minute warning. If you're on borrowed time, it's still worthwhile to have adults write for three minutes. You may be amazed with how fast God speaks when his people are listening and focused.

Take time for all the participants to share something about their experiences. Tell them the total amount of time the group has for sharing and each person has for sharing. If you know some people won't stick to a minute or two, set a timer and gently move on to the next person as needed. After doing this a time or two, people learn how to keep it shorter.

I've found that I can't be in a small group myself while I'm leading with a timer. I try to listen at more than one table so I have a better picture of how things are going. This helps me know if people are staying on the surface or sharing deeply so I can help move them forward in their conversations.

DIALOGUE PRAYER

I first started journaling my prayers by simply talking to God in my journal as if he were sitting in front of me. I would start by chatting or complaining, and I often found myself asking him a question. This is how the profound experience of meeting God face-to-face through my journals occurred. It's also why writing one verse a day became a large part of my spiritual practice. God regularly gave me a verse that answered a question.

At first I didn't know it was a way God would speak to me directly. And I didn't notice him doing it at first. That made it even more real for me when I discovered he was talking to me all along. When I was single, I felt that Jesus was my husband. I talked to him every day, and he cared about everything I wanted to talk about, so we dialogued. It wasn't one-sided.

On your own before you lead

Take a moment to think about something you would like to share with Jesus, and write it down. Cry out to him if you need to. Ask him a question if you feel you need an answer. Write down one verse from Scripture. Use a reference book with specific verses in the Bible on specific topics, or look up verses in a concordance. If you think it won't distract you much, use a Bible app or simply use a Bible reading method you're already using.

Leading Dialogue Prayer

Put out paper or journals, pens, Bibles, and reference books with specific verses in the Bible on specific topics.

Encourage the group to talk directly to God about what is going on in their hearts and minds at the time. Also suggest they ask God a question. Have them read Scripture or write out a passage of Scripture they feel God wants them to hear.

Debrief by asking questions about what the process was like for them. Ask what was hard or easy about it and what God seemed to be saying to them in the process.

THE PRAYER OF EXAMEN

St. Ignatius was born in 1491 into a large, wealthy family. He was wounded in war as a young man and was bedridden in his brother's castle for a long time. He began to daydream about worldly things to pass the time. The daydreams granted pleasure in the moment but left him depressed. As Ignatius was recovering, he began reading about the life of Christ and day-dreaming about what it would be like to follow him. These thoughts not only gave him great pleasure in the moment but continued to bring him great joy.

Out of the time Ignatius spent in bed, he created the prayer of examen as a thirty-day time of refection in solitude.

Over the years, followers of Christ have found this prayer helpful as a daily reflection on their lives in and among people. I fell in love with it even before I knew about Ignatius and the prayer of examen, and it was already a part of my journaling practice. I was finding as a single woman I needed someone to process my day with, so each night before I would go to sleep, I sat in bed and told Jesus all about my day. I also told him what had happened during the past twenty-four hours. Anything I thought was interesting, difficult, funny, or hard, I offered up to

God. I let God know what I was thankful for and what had hurt or frustrated me. Over the years, I inadvertently documented my life with Christ—the good, the bad, and the ugly.

Not only did I love the intimate moments I had with Jesus each night before I went to bed, I also processed how I wanted to live more fully aligned with him the next day. I saw where I wasn't living according to how he was calling me. I saw him at work as I wrote and processed. I normally dwelled way too long on certain things, but this process helped me leave it all at the foot of the cross so I could move on the next day into what God was calling me to.

Now that I'm married, I know it's important to share most things with my husband, but there are some things he doesn't need to hear. Just ten minutes of journaling can save a whole day of hurt and frustration for me and those around me.

To do the prayer of examen, rewind the past twenty-four hours of your life in your mind. Let them play like a movie in your head. Notice things that stir up emotion. Ask yourself some questions: *When did I feel most fully alive today? When did I feel the lifeblood draining out of me? Who drew me closer to Christ? Who seemed to pull me away from him?*

Be aware of the presence of God. Even picture yourself and Jesus watching your day together. As you watch, see what he has to say about your day. Name one thing you wish you'd done or not done over the course of the day. Then talk to God about the next day.

Leading the Prayer of Examen

Provide paper and pen for participants. Encourage them to sit comfortably in their chairs, to close their eyes, and to try to find themselves sitting in the presence of God. Encourage them to take a few deep breaths.

After a moment of silence, ask them to think back twenty-four hours from the present. Ask, "Where were you? What were you doing? Who were you with? See if you can create a movie in your mind of your last twenty-four hours."

Sometimes I give prompts if I think the group is struggling. I may say, "Yesterday at this time, you may have just finished dinner, or you were really hungry because you hadn't gotten to eat dinner yet." Or I may name the times, hour by hour, to keep people on track and moving through their twenty-four hours. As always, discern what your group needs in the moment.

After you've taken a few minutes to let people watch their day go by, prompt them with at least one question from each category below.

Giving thanks for the presence of God:

- In the past twenty-four hours, when did you feel most fully alive?
- What happened in the past twenty-four hours that you're most thankful for?
- In the past twenty-four hours, who drew you closer to Christ?
- In the past twenty-four hours, when did you feel closest to God?
- When were you fully aware of God's presence?
- How was God there for you today?
- In what way(s) did you feel drawn to God today?
- Who or what is plugging you back into the presence of God?

Becoming aware of not seeing God in your life:

- In the past twenty-four hours, when did the lifeblood drain out of you?
- In the past twenty-four hours, who seemed to pull you away from God?

▦ When did you pull away from Christ in the past twenty-four hours?

▦ In the past twenty-four hours, when did you feel farthest from God?

▦ Name a moment when you weren't thinking about God.

Repenting:

▦ Name one thing in the past twenty-four hours that you wish you had done or not done.

▦ What's one way you believe you let God down?

▦ What's one way you think you let someone else down?

▦ Do you need to apologize to someone you've wronged in the past twenty-four hours? If so, plan to do it.

▦ Share something you wish you'd done differently in the past twenty-four hours.

Moving forward into the presence of God:

▦ Having done this process, write down one thing about to-morrow that comes to mind.

▦ Ask God for what you need for the next twenty-four hours.

▦ Share how you hope tomorrow will be different than today was.

▦ Share how you hope to see God in the next twenty-four hours.

Write your questions for this practice according to the theme of your retreat, youth group night, Sunday morning worship, or other gathering. Crafting the questions to match the theme of the day may help the group connect with the questions more. It also may help people remember to ask themselves these questions after the event as they're reflecting on the experience they had there. If they have a T-shirt or other take-home of some sort with the theme on it, it could remind them to do some of the prayer of examen questions you adapted to fit the theme.

I'm always looking for ways to bolster others' long-term relationship with Christ. I lead not just to teach a practice like the prayer of examen but also so participants can enter into the presence of God on their own later. My hope is that they learn to feed themselves rather than needing to be spoon-fed by others. It takes babies a lot of practice with a parent helping them eat before they're able to do the whole process on their own. So each time you're preparing to lead a spiritual practice, focus on the long-term goal of them being able to practice it on their own.

Do a short check in with your group by doing thumbs-up, thumbs-down. As your family is around the dinner table, as your church council is meeting, or as you connect at the beginning of Sunday school, encourage everyone to put their thumbs up and share one good thing that's happened since the last time you all were together. Then have them put their thumbs down to share one thing that was hard or bad.

This idea works with anyone from kids as young as four to adults, who may be getting less and less verbal. The gesture of thumbs up and thumbs down communicates much, so not as many words are needed.

TWO PRACTICES FOR GROUPS

On retreats, before board meetings, during Sunday school, in a college classroom, or in a preschool classroom, the following practices, Pick a Picture and Use a Timeline, can encourage people to engage in spiritual conversations together. Both of them work well around tables. As leaders, we tend not to go deep when we're having conversations about our lives, but these practices can give us opportunities to give our greatest gifts to each another.

Pick a Picture. Get people talking about their life by having them pick a picture and share how it reveals where they're at spiritually. Here's how to have pictures available:

- Take pictures and print them out for participants to choose from. This works great for three reasons: it's low cost, participants can take the pictures with them, and you can connect the pictures to a theme, if desired.

- Some companies sell packs of pictures for group use. Youth Specialties sells some called "Every Picture Tells a Story."

- Have participants pick a picture on their phone. Be careful with this one though. Our phones take us to a whole other world when we open them, and we can forget about the people in the room as we engage with life outside the room instead. However, the younger generation has gotten good at showing each other what's on their phones and dialoguing with each other at the same time.

- Cut out magazine pictures. Make sure to cut out just images, as titles, articles, and other words can be distractions.

If you think your group needs to warm up to the idea of spiritual conversations, have each of them pick a picture that shares how they're feeling *in general*, not spiritually. Each time you use this process, add something a little more spiritual in nature to help them get into deeper spiritual conversations. Try to choose pictures that will connect with your specific group and in the direction you want the group to be going spiritually.

At the beginning of a group's time together, pictures can give participants a moment to reflect on where they're at with God. Consider using pictures as a way to introduce a lesson. End a session with them as a way to check in with how people are doing spiritually before everyone departs.

Use a Timeline. Another way to process life is to draw a timeline and then discuss it with each other. Take a moment to think about your past and your future at the same time. Encourage participants to draw a timeline with the center being *NOW*. The first part is the past, and the other side is the future. Remind participants that none of us can see the future. God encourages us not to worry about tomorrow, because tomorrow has enough trouble of its own (Matthew 6:34). However, he does say that "your old men will dream dreams, your young men will see visions" (Joel 2:28). God wants us to reflect on the past so we can move forward in our lives according to his love and purposes.

One day in a women's Bible study, I was encouraging a group of women to use a timeline, and I suddenly realized how difficult that would be for our blind member. I found some rocks and clay so she could create a timeline as well. Her group came alive, asking her questions about her life and about how God was at work in her.

6

ACTIVE PRAYER *with* ONE ANOTHER

At my church, we have three full-time staff members. Once a year, the three of us spend one day not far from our church, thinking about what God has for our church for the year. Each of us plans two hours of the day. Our favorite part has become walking along a river for about an hour, praying for specific people in our congregation. As we walk, we let names, faces, and families come to mind, and we pray out loud. There's something powerful about praying for people out loud in God's creation, with onlookers assuming we're only talking to each other.

I like active prayer because it gives active people a way to engage fully with the living God. It can connect people of all ages, races, and genders in tangible ways as they engage their bodies. They also can be adapted for those with physical limitations. Each activity gives space to be active while talking to each other and the living God. None requires reading or writing, which makes them accessible across language and literacy barriers.

We once set up a prayer walk around a pavilion in Nicaragua. We put a sign on each pole of the pavilion, most of which had just a word or two in both English and Spanish—for example, *family, school, work, community*. We then mixed our English speakers with our Spanish speakers and spent about thirty minutes walking around the pavilion, praying in our own language.

When I was on a different mission trip, the group leader told us to ask God who we were to pray for and then to go pray for that person. A face came to mind, and I searched the crowd. She wasn't there. Then I remembered I'd seen her lying down in a room about an hour before, so I made my way to that room, found her, and prayed for her.

Later a college student on the trip asked, "What happens when you don't find the person God put on your heart?" I laughed and told her what had happened for me. In the next moment, we were all told to board a bus and to pray with people near us. Lo and behold, the person on her heart was sitting right next to us. If I hadn't done the practice with the group, I may not have been able to guide those I was leading.

THE SPIRITUAL AND BIBLICAL
PERSPECTIVE ON ACTIVE PRAYER

Jesus revealed himself in Scripture in an active way. He didn't just go around teaching people how to think; his ministry was physical and active. It involved people's bodies as well as their minds. Throughout the Gospels, Jesus can be found walking with people and engaging them in conversations. His signs, wonders, and teachings often involved the physical realm. When he healed a man who couldn't walk, he said, "Take

your mat and walk" (Mark 2:9). He walked on water and encouraged Peter to walk on water as well. He called the twelve
disciples saying, "Come follow me" (Matthew 19:21; Mark 1:17;
Luke 18:22). He challenged the Pharisees who were about to
stone a woman caught in adultery, saying, "Let any one of you
who is without sin be the first to throw a stone at her" (John 8:7).

This chapter will help you engage others in both their
physical beings and their spiritual beings. The practices can
help participants engage with God not just in their minds but
also as they experience the physical world around them. God
created the physical world we live in, and it's one of the main
ways he reveals himself to us even today. My hope is that you
have the opportunity to introduce people you're leading to a
deeper walk with Christ as they experience God in their
physical activity.

Throughout church history, churches have brought different
physical expressions of worship into their own settings. The
liturgical church is known for their many physical expressions
of worship, such as kneeling, bowing, using incense, wearing
robes, and carrying crosses. Charismatic Christians raise their
hands and move as they worship. No matter what church you're
a part of or what your comfort level is with physical expressions
of worship, we are all physical beings in the presence of God.

PARABLE WALK

When Jesus walked the earth, he pointed out everyday things
and then shared a deep truth. In chapter thirteen of the book
of Matthew, we find Jesus climbing onto a boat then sharing
parables about farmers, seeds, and weeds. Each time I read one
of Christ's parables, I'm impressed how he chose things to talk
about that still exist over two thousand years later, so the truth
is still relevant today.

On a parable walk, you imagine Jesus is walking with you, and he wants to teach you something from what you see as you walk. The first time I did a parable walk, I went solo on top of a large hill. It was beautiful. Since that California experience, I've had many more great parable walks, even inside buildings when the weather wasn't conducive to being outside.

As I walked that first time, right away a song I'd known for years came to mind. At first I hummed it as I wandered slowly toward some running water. God said something so clearly to me, I thought, *I will never forget this amazing moment.* Then I turned, and there was a path where Jesus talked to me about something else. For thirty minutes, at each turn Jesus told me things I never would have heard sitting still. That time of prayer was unique, because I was seeing something new each moment as I walked. It was as if Jesus was pointing things out to me, sharing biblical truths with me. If I had been sitting still with my eyes closed, I wouldn't have seen those things.

As that walk came to a close, I longed for more. I wanted to stay in that intimate time with God, yet I also wanted to share with my group all that God had revealed to me along the way. I had found a new delightful way to communicate with God, and I felt fully alive.

I've shared this parable walk concept with hundreds of people since then. Each time I lead a group through the process, I'm excited to see how God moves. One night I decided to lead this practice after dark under a full moon. Almost everyone focused on that moon, and everyone heard something different from God. We all experienced profoundly beautiful moments in the dark, in the church parking lot.

Recently, as I was leading this spiritual practice with a group of women, I invited them to sketch or watercolor the main thing God had them reflect on during their parable walk. I sometimes encourage people to document by taking a photo as they walk, listen, and process. Having photos in the debriefing session helps people share their experience. It's also a way to engage technology in people's spiritual lives. Some people post their photos on social media to show what God is doing. A friend of mine takes it up a notch and gives people empty frames to look through to help them focus on the main thing Jesus is pointing out to them.

Leading a Parable Walk

Introduce this practice by reading a few short parables. Tell participants Jesus used parables to help people understand the kingdom of God. Say something like this: "Today I'm going to give you thirty minutes to walk and talk with Jesus. As you leave this space, imagine you're walking with him, and he's pointing out things as you walk."

Encourage them to focus on what they notice and to ask Jesus what he has to teach them. Tell them that as they're focusing, they can take a picture of it on their phone, sketch it, or paint it. They don't have to be artists but are simply trying to capture what God is trying to say to them through what they sketch or photograph. Encourage them not to worry about what the final product looks like, but emphasize what God is revealing to them in the moment.

Allow them to spend a few more moments focusing on the revelation, such as by adding color to a drawing with watercolors. As they're reflecting, suggest they find a title for their art or find a passage of Scripture and reflect on it. Say something like, "Wherever or however God leads you during this time, follow."

Ask them to come back together, then lead a time of sharing for a few minutes, first in small groups and then as a whole group, as time allows.

USING A LABYRINTH

In Old Testament times, followers of God were expected to journey to the temple three times a year to honor him (Exodus 34:23-24). Over time, when Christian followers couldn't journey all the way to Jerusalem for different reasons, they used labyrinths to make the journey—at least in their hearts. Labyrinths are a way for Christians to walk and pray and take time to hear from God. As believers live farther and farther away from Jerusalem, we walk labyrinths as a way to still honor the journey that honored God.

One of the first labyrinths in a Christian church was created in AD 325. Christians have generally thought about the labyrinth journey in two different ways: as Jesus' journey to the cross and as a journey to the temple to atone for their sins. Some people even journey a labyrinth on their knees to show the depth of their sinfulness or to align themselves with Christ in his sacrifice for them on the cross.

When I introduce the prayer labyrinth to people, I let them know there are no rules; the purpose is to have a dialogue with God. I encourage people to talk to God but also to listen. Practicing in a dialogue journal before leading will help you understand this concept.

If we're using an indoor canvas labyrinth, before people start walking the labyrinth, I encourage them to remove their shoes to remind them they are about to walk on holy ground. You can buy beautiful prayer labyrinths, or you can create your own on a cloth tarp.

One day, as I was on a local mission trip with my church, I came around the corner to find a tarp prayer labyrinth cut in half and being used to catch paint. I took it to our church and taped it back together. One morning, when I was using the labyrinth for a women's Bible study, a woman walked into the room, overwhelmed with sorrow. She said her father, who had painted houses for a living, wasn't going to be walking at her daughter's wedding that summer because he was not walking well anymore and was in a wheelchair. As she entered the room with the labyrinth, she stopped dead in her tracks. I had put rose petals on the floor leading up to the labyrinth that day. She walked the labyrinth in her stocking feet. She shared with her group about how many times she and her dad had walked on paint tarps together over the years. She suddenly wasn't feeling just the presence of God but also the peace that her dad would be present even if he wasn't walking down the aisle. No matter where a labyrinth is, what it looks like, or what it's made of, God loves to reveal himself to people through it.

Encourage participants to talk to God on the way in to the center of the labyrinth and to listen to God on the way out. Or participants can think of a question they have for God. As they walk, they can allow him to speak. Sometimes I end up in a dialogue with God as I walk, going back and forth with him, listening for what he has to say as I make each turn.

It's good to do the parable walk with your group before you do the labyrinth, because a labyrinth provides a parable. For example, when we feel close to finishing or close to the center, we imagine God is sitting or standing, waiting for us. But suddenly the path takes us far from him, and we feel distant, unable to return to his side on our own power. So the labyrinth is a way to seek to be near to the heart of God.

One day I was using the prayer labyrinth in the class that included a blind woman, and I realized she wouldn't be able to do it. But then the woman who brought her stood in front of her and said, "Put your hand on my shoulder," and led her through the entire prayer labyrinth. This was a profound moment for me as I watched the beauty unfold and prayed for the woman who was leading. Both she and I have the spiritual gift of helping, a gift that can land us in a place of always helping others and not taking time for ourselves to be present to God.

One of the other women in our group said she would bring her wooden finger labyrinth, which was meant to be used with eyes closed. The next week, we all watched as our blind friend moved her finger through the labyrinth. It's powerful to see the body of Christ come alongside people and adapt things as needed.

PRAYER WALK

I have done several kinds of prayer walks over the years, mostly on mission trips. When I was first introduced to the concept, we walked two by two and prayed out loud. At first it was very uncomfortable for me. I was young and afraid that I may look dumb. So each time I introduce the concept of prayer walking, I name how awkward it can feel. And I remind participants that most of us walk and talk to each other without looking crazy, and no one but us knows we're praying. Once I was able to get past worrying about what people thought, I started to see the things I needed to be praying for. As we walked, we prayed. As we prayed, we saw how God specifically answered prayer.

The power of prayer walking is that you and your partner later see the work of God. Seeing answers to prayer is two-fold: first, if we don't pray, we can't say the outcome was an answer to prayer; second, because we're walking side by side, we both are witnesses to what God is doing and has done. Without one another, we rarely even remember the things we've prayed for, and therefore we forget to give God the glory for the work he has done.

Jesus walked and talked often (for example, see Luke 9:57). A specific practice called the Emmaus walk also gives people the space to walk and talk together and will again draw you into the heart of God as well as connect you deeply spiritually to one another.

Sometimes we do a prayer walk specifically for the community we're walking in. As we're walking and praying for that community, we let things we see trigger what God wants us to pray for. We've done a few prayer walks in our community while passing out flyers inviting people to our church or to a garage sale with a purpose. I've prayed for families by name when they have a rock or other item in their lawn with their names on it. We also pray that God gives us opportunities to share the gospel. Sometimes we walk and pray for something specific for our church. Sometimes we pray for the person we're walking with.

Leading a Prayer Walk

Ask everyone to find a partner, because you don't want anyone to feel left out and because you can use this as a strategic moment to build connections. You can choose to put people together that don't know each other very well, or you might know that someone could really benefit from connecting with someone specific. Two by two works best for hearing and for walking on most sidewalks. Help people find partners as needed.

Let everyone know specifically what they can be praying for as they walk. For example, if you're starting a new ministry in a neighborhood, the group can walk that neighborhood and pray for it according to what and who they see as they walk.

Tell them that it enhances the practice to pray out loud so they hear one another praying and so they can later be a witness to how God answered their prayers. Don't forget to add where to walk and when to return. Then pray for them as a sendoff.

Try not to busy yourself with tasks as they walk. Instead, walk and pray with them. This will help during the debriefing. If you walk with the group, you will see what they see along the path. If something happens while people are out on the prayer walk, you will experience it with them and can talk about it at the end of the walk. I also like to participate so I can express both what was hard and what was good about the process for me. It helps other people feel like they can say what was good and bad about the prayer walk as well.

Upon return, debrief the prayer walk. Ask what the experience was like for them. What came to mind to pray for on the walk? What was different about praying and walking than if they'd stayed inside to pray? Was there anything that surprised them as they walked and prayed with their partner?

Long-term follow-up can be powerful. If you're praying for an event, have people share answers to prayer after the event. If you're praying for a long-term initiative, create an environment where people can share answers to prayer along the way. When we take the time to recall answered prayer together, we get to see the hand of God together.

EMMAUS WALK

Find a walking partner you desire to have a deeper conversation with, someone who's willing to walk at your pace. For those who are unable to walk, an Emmaus walk can be adapted to a sitting exercise. I've also done this practice with a person present via Skype. I encourage those who can't walk not to be discouraged, because it will still be a fruitful practice. When I schedule an Emmaus walk for a retreat but the weather doesn't cooperate, we do the walk inside a building.

Before we leave the room, I encourage walking partners to sit next to each other. Then we read Luke 24:13-35, the story of the road to Emmaus, together as a group. This is an account of what took place after Christ rose from the dead, when some didn't yet know he had risen. As I read this story, I encourage participants to enter in using a Scripture technique that combines truth and imagination. Each person imagines who she is in the story and how close or far she is from Jesus. I then ask participants to engage all five of their senses, noticing what they see, hear, touch, taste, and smell as they find themselves on the road to Emmaus.

Leading an Emmaus Walk

First read Luke 24:13-35, asking the group to pretend they're looking around at the sights along the road. Pause for a moment so everyone can take the story in. Ask, "What stood out to you?"

Ask participants to turn to their walking partner and share what stood out to them about the story so far. Before the groups depart for their walks, ask each table or small group to share a main theme that came up within their group.

Point out that this passage recalls a seven-mile walk. Jesus and the two men had lots of time to walk and talk as they went. The men also didn't recognize Jesus. Remind the participants they're going to take a thirty-minute walk with their partner. Tell them that as they walk, they'll each get a chance to talk about what's concerning them, just like the men in this story. Suggest that they discuss their disappointments, hopes, dreams, and expectations.

Encourage them to consider the fact that Jesus is walking alongside them and that he may have something to add to the dialogue. Tell them, "If either of you notices a place in the conversation when you think Jesus may interject, try to verbalize that in the conversation, saying something like, 'I wonder what Jesus may say to you right now?' As you share, notice if you experienced Christ walking with you when the moment being discussed originally occurred, or if you recognized the presence of Christ only afterward, or if you're still trying to understand where God was or is in your life."

Though Jesus knew everything that had happened, he still asked them questions. He knew the men needed to talk about it and process his death. In this world of social media, when we come together, we often already know what's going on in each other's lives—or so we think. Encourage the participants to take a page out of Jesus' book by asking their walking partner about his or her life, even if they think they already know.

Encourage the walkers to be aware of the time as they walk, giving each other ten minutes to share what's heavy on their hearts. Have someone set a ten-minute timer on their phone to help them stay on time. After the first person shares for ten minutes, the pair should talk for five minutes back and forth, allowing space to wonder what Jesus may say in the conversation. Then they each can take five minutes to pray about the situation out loud.

Gather the group and debrief. Ask them to share only their own story so they don't disclose private information. Ask questions like these:

▦ What was hard or easy about this practice?

▦ How did Jesus show up for you during this time?

▦ How might you use this concept as you move forward in this part of your life?

EXERCISE CLASS

I started doing yoga in my thirties. I was a little worried about the spiritual element to it, so I found ways to connect with Jesus in class. At the beginning of each class, I dwelled on something

Christ focused, such as gaining the peace that only Christ can offer. Often I went to yoga on my sabbath, so it was a part of honoring God fully as I physically entered into deep physical rest with him. At the start of each class, I chose a breath prayer I needed that day. One day, as I was doing each move, I found myself worshiping God as I went into each pose.

One of my friends, a spiritual director, told me she uses motions while praying the Lord's Prayer, so I added my own poses to the Lord's Prayer, one for each section. At the next retreat, they had hired a yoga instructor to lead yoga in the afternoon, so I taught them the Lord's Prayer moves.

That same year, a woman at my church said she felt called to lead yoga for free at our church and asked if I would consider it. She and I led the class for multiple seasons, adding more and more yoga moves that she required me to rename as something Christ centered.

We had a great time laughing and worshiping God with our bodies in that class. We even had a few visitors worship Christ with us. Instead of having an intention at the beginning of class, we had a verse for the day. Every Tuesday night we created a breath prayer from the verse, started the worship music, and worshiped God using the different yoga poses. It was wonderful to feel fully alive both physically and spiritually as we ended our time each Tuesday.

The following lists the poses I connected to the Lord's Prayer, but please remember to be creative and to let God move. For it is in Christ that we move and have our being (Acts 17:28).

Work at your own pace, and use alternate poses as you wish. Listen to your body, and take breaks if needed. If you feel pain, stop and take a break. Rejoin the group when you're ready.

THE LORD'S PRAYER WITH YOUR BODY

Our Father in heaven (extended mountain pose),

hallowed be your name (downward dog),

your kingdom come (warrior pose),

your will be done (triangle pose),

on earth (child pose) as it is in heaven (tree pose).

Give us today our daily bread (cobra).

And forgive us our debts (forward fold),

as we also forgive our debtors (mountain pose back bend).

And lead us not into temptation (warrior three),

but deliver us from the evil one (high lunge).

(Matthew 6:9-13)

For thine is the kingdom and the power (plank)

and the glory forever and ever (chair pose),

amen (hands together in prayer pose).

Here are some additional poses to use:

- tangled in sin (eagle pose)
- looking to Jesus (seated spine twist)
- resist the devil and he will flee (side plank)
- meditating on the Word (pigeon pose)
- Sea of Galilee (boat pose)
- sabbath rest (corpse pose)

The naming of these poses came when I just paused, meditated, and listened for the Holy Spirit. After I had connected poses with the Lord's Prayer over months of listening, the rest of them came quickly during class. For example, one day my coinstructor said, "Okay, we're going to do cat/cow pose now."

I said what popped into my mind: "Swayback donkey, and camel." We burst out laughing, and it stuck.

We had small prayer cards each week with our verse for the day on them. As we were all meditating on the Word in the pigeon pose, the senior pastor lifted his head with the Word of God at the front of his mind—literally. One of the cards was stuck on his sweaty forehead.

Being active takes the solemnness out of prayer—in a good way. It allows us to be playful with God in prayer. God is whimsical and fun, and we often forget this when we're entering into prayer with him. Just look at all the beauty, whimsy, and fun in creation. Take his lead, have fun, enter in, and use your full body to worship Jesus today.

USING THESE PRACTICES

Here are some ways to be creative in active prayer:

- at retreats, especially when teaching how to notice God in creation
- in the middle of a board meeting when there's a need to be prayerful or to get unstuck
- with middle school students, who are very active yet want to engage quietly with God
- on mission trips as a way to pray together for the work you're doing together
- during Bible studies, to help people get outside the box when praying and studying the Scriptures
- to teach mentors, such as Stephen Ministers, as a new way to listen and pray with others
- on marriage retreats or with summer staff at a camp, to bring participants to new depths in caring and in praying for one another

SHARING LIFE *on* LIFE

WHEN I WAS A CHILD, I didn't know that my grandfather was a strong believer. He smoked cigars and didn't attend church regularly. In my young mind, there was no way he could know Christ as Savior. He never breathed a word about his personal relationship with Christ to me until I was a junior in college, when I added youth ministry as a minor to my education. Suddenly monthly one-page handwritten letters arrived from my grandfather, sharing with me his life in ministry.

The story began with him traveling with his father from church to church in England as his father led choirs. One day, when he was fifteen, a group of traveling evangelists from Cliff Bible College came to one of those churches and led him to the Lord. When it was time to head off to college, he wanted to attend that school, but he had the privilege of going there for only a year before it closed because of World War II. However, he had been trained well in a year's time, learning the Scriptures and going on foot to share the gospel.

When he was expected to head off to war, he refused to carry a weapon, so he was invited to become a traveling pastor in churches without pastors, as they too were drafted. He served faithfully for years in multiple churches in England, even after the war was over. He then began taking his son, my father, from church to church as he preached.

My grandfather, with his wife and two sons, immigrated to Canada and then on to the United States when my father was a teenager. Upon arrival, my grandfather's spiritual gifts were met with a mixed reception in the churches of America. Before I was born, there had been one too many rejections from a church, and my grandfather was done with church forever—not done with Jesus, but done with being hurt by the church, never to engage with ministry again, besides telling me about my spiritual heritage.

Just two years after I started ministry, my grandfather passed away from brain cancer, leaving me with many questions. But I'm thankful for the spiritual legacy he gave me in the last four years of his life. He always closed his letters with the words, "Keep the Faith," and that is what he taught me. Keep the faith and share your faith!

SHARING WORDS OF ENCOURAGEMENT

If you're seeking to build community, I hope this chapter—actually this whole book—helps to take your group deeper together. Words of encouragement in written form, like those my grandfather shared with me, are a powerful way to share your faith while you're alive and can also last beyond your own lifetime.

Words of encouragement can also go beyond family, creating deep relationships and deep faith sharing. Writing words of encouragement is a great way to bond a group together and to honor God. My church has done this on mission trips as we have spoken words of affirmation to each other at the end of the day, presented a bead to add to a bracelet, tied fabric around wrists, written notes to one another, or put one person in the middle of the circle each night. Families have written letters to people who are going on a mission trip so we can take those letters for them to read when their spirits are low. Whatever a group's role is, it always helps to build healthy community within it.

The Emmaus walk (chapter six) is a spiritual practice done with other people as well. I recommend trying it in small groups as well as large groups.

Find ways you can try some of these practices in worship on Sunday mornings or when opening meetings. Mission trips are really conducive to most of these practices. They can be used as a devotional moment or as a part of the ministry work. Consider engaging those you're ministering *to*, not just those you're ministering *with*. I have used all of these in the Bible study groups I lead.

Recently a staff member wanted to have a worship night with her young-adult group in my home, using spiritual practices as a way for them to engage deeply with God and one another. We picked a night and got the lighting vibe just right. She led an acoustic worship set with her husband, and I led a few of the practices from this book. It was different from the usual worship service, where everyone faces forward; they turned toward each other as they engaged with God and shared what he was doing in and through them that night. And they engaged with each other on a deep emotional and spiritual level.

THE SPIRITUAL AND BIBLICAL PERSPECTIVE ON SHARING LIFE IN COMMUNITY

The early Christian church shared life. As you read the letters of Paul to the churches, you can see that they engaged in life together. Sometimes it was positive, and sometimes it was negative, which means they were doing a lot of life sharing. Paul addressed things such as division, immoral behavior, lawsuits, sexual immorality, marriage, food, freedom, property, money, spiritual gifts, worship, and Christ's death and resurrection—and that's just in the first letter to the Corinthians. He reminded them that they all must know each other and work together to be the body of Christ. When we share from our real lives, we're living into what Christ desired for his church: a deep spiritual connection.

Since the practices in this chapter are done in community, trying them on your own first is tricky. Read the practice all the way through, and try to engage with it yourself and with God before you lead it with a group. Dwell in the Word can be done with as few as four people, so you can practice beforehand with four people.

GROUP SPIRITUAL DIRECTION

Spiritual direction is the act of listening for the Holy Spirit in the presence of others. A spiritual director's role is to listen on behalf of the directee to what God is saying and doing in the directee's life. In formal spiritual direction, the spiritual director does 90 percent of the listening. During that hour or so, the two seek to hear from God together.

By engaging in the spiritual practices in this chapter, you and those you lead are doing a form of spiritual direction with one another. Listen to one another, and notice what God is doing in your lives. Be aware that this is only an introduction to group spiritual direction, a truncated way to do listening groups so that this concept is accessible to a larger population than just those committed to long-term groups that meet regularly.

DWELL IN THE WORD

To Dwell in the Word—by simply reading a passage of Scripture— is a way to enter into the Scriptures together deeply, asking one or two questions about the passage and sharing thoughts about it with a partner. Then the pair tells another pair what they heard from their partner.

I was first introduced to the Dwell in the Word spiritual practice around a table full of pastors. The pastor leading the practice was extremely smart, and I was a little intimidated, to say the least. As he began to explain the practice, I found myself freaking out on the inside yet pretending to be calm, cool, and collected. I feared I'd do the practice wrong or say something stupid about the Scriptures. I just didn't want to do it. Thankfully, somehow I was able to enter in, and by the end I had a newfound spiritual practice that I loved.

As leaders of spiritual practices, we can't always do what we want to do; we can't lead and practice at the same time. When you are leading, always be ready to participate so that you have the right number of people in each group. Because I'm the leader or pastor in the room, sometimes my words overpower others simply because they assume my answer is the only answer. The pastor or leader is in authority during sermons and teaching sessions, but that's not so in spiritual practices. You want each person to listen for what God is saying to him or her as an individual. While practicing Dwell in the Word, we often learn from one another as peers.

Simply put, Dwell in the Word is taking time to slow down, read Scripture together in community, and discuss it. As you start the practice, you simply read and listen to the passage first without any explanation. After you've read the Scripture once, you find a partner and read it again. Once you've read it a second time, you have time to discuss it with your partner before you discuss the passage with a larger group.

Leading Dwell in the Word

Preparation

Choose a passage of Scripture you'd like the group to focus on or learn from. This passage can be one that you're using for a weekend retreat or that will be read in worship or that you know your group would benefit from reading and discussing. Choosing the length of the passage based on how much time you have and the age or attention span of your group. Ten verses is a good amount for most groups. If you're crunched for time or you have a young group, cut that number in half.

For this practice you can use *any* type of passage. It can be a story, psalm, or proverb. If you really want to use a certain passage with a spiritual practice, but it doesn't work well with imaginative prayer or lectio divina, try it with Dwell in the Word.

Once you've chosen the passage, print it out so everyone has the same version of Scripture and can take notes right on the paper, if desired. I also sometimes print out questions that are a part of the practice to help people track with the process.

During

Read the passage out loud and have the group listen and follow along. Pause for a minute of silence after the passage has been read. Let them know you pause to allow them to process.

Before you read the passage the second time, tell them they'll be seeking to answer one of these two questions:

- Where does your imagination go when you read this passage?

- What would you ask a biblical scholar about this passage?

After reading the passage again, encourage them to jot down a few notes answering one of these two questions about the passage. Give a minute or two of silence to do this task.

After the silence, encourage the group to look for a friendly stranger. The idea is that you'd like them to find someone in the group they don't know very well.

As they find that person, ask them to introduce themselves to one another. Depending on your group, you could encourage them to share something funny about themselves or something a little deeper. For example, if it's a group of junior high boys, have them share the craziest noise they can make; if it is a group of adults in worship, encourage them to share one grounding fact about themselves that could provoke conversation at a later date—for example, I have three children, or I am from Texas, or my favorite exercise is sit-ups.

After short introductions, maybe just thirty seconds each, the next step is explaining how the rest of the spiritual practice will go. Say something like this: "For the next two minutes, one of you in your pair will share about this passage, answering one of the questions without interruption. The person listening can jot down notes, nod, say ummm, and use good eye contact. Do not ask any questions or add anything to what the person is saying. When it's your turn to listen, really listen, because you're going to have to give a summary of what your partner said to someone else in a few minutes. If you have a poor memory, jot down a few notes. If that was a lot of information to remember, don't worry. I'll walk you through each step."

Set a timer for two minutes. If you're working with a group of ministry professionals with this particular spiritual practice, I encourage you to give them three to four minutes. High school students and younger may be able to do this for only one minute.

Tell the groups to decide who's going to share first and who's going to listen first. If you have a young or distracted group, prompt with saying, "Raise your hand if you're speaking first."

No matter what age, I usually say, "Ready, set, go," so everyone knows to get started at the same time. It's easier for people to start sharing if all the voices in the room start at the same time.

At the end of the two minutes, say, "Switch," so everyone can hear, and then tell them to give the other person two minutes to share uninterrupted. Say, "Ready, set, go, and remember to listen well." Sometimes participants try to finish their thought *after* the end of two minutes, but it's important that you help the whole group move to the next person. This practice is great for training over-talkers to be concise and under-talkers to get the same amount of airtime. It's also a great spiritual discipline to teach a group with different amounts of expertise in the Scriptures.

After both people have shared, give them thirty seconds or so to jot down or look over notes they've taken.

Tell the groups they need to find another pair of people to become a group of four—or six if there is one extra pair. Then have them go around their group introducing their partner and sharing what their partner said about the passage of Scripture. For many, this is intimidating at first, so encourage them to do their best. Remind them they're doing only a summary, not repeating every word, so it should take only about thirty seconds.

Let them know it will be tempting to help the other person remember what was said or to add to it to make sure he gives all the information. Instead encourage them to thank their partner and let him know he did a good job. It may also be tempting to add to what you think the person might have said or might have meant, but it's important to share only what was actually said. This shows good listening skills, an important spiritual discipline that has become a lost art.

After

Once all the groups have shared, it's good to ask the group as a whole what they learned or gleaned from the process. I usually say something like, "It's fun to hear from so many different people about what they got out of the same passage of Scripture." Often I then remind them the Word of God is living and active and can teach us new things if we let it transform us each time we read it.

If you have time, use any of the debriefing questions from the first chapter. Also, if you're looking to dig deeper into the passage of Scripture, spend a lot more time asking what people learned from reading it twice, talking about it, and listening to what other people heard from God. This practice can greatly enrich discussion in your groups. It also can fill an entire lesson time if you slow it down and dwell longer in each section. It's a great introduction to teaching on the passage as well.

Remember to be creative. For example, change some of the questions. If you're focusing on evangelism, you may ask, "What would you tell a nonbeliever about this passage?" or "What may someone far from God ask about this passage?" or "If you had to explain this passage to someone who had never read the Bible before, what would you say?" These are just ideas to get you thinking. Remember, you're created in the image of God, and he is the Creator, so you are creative in some way, shape, or form. See if you can tap into your God-given creativity as you think about how you can adapt this practice. I recommend doing it the way I've outlined the first few times so you feel comfortable with the rhythm of the practice before you make any big adaptations. No matter what, have fun, because if you have fun, so will your group.

THE NINETY-SECOND TESTIMONY

One of the most transformative spiritual practices is simply sharing parts of your spiritual story. I remember the first time I shared a part of my spiritual story with a group. I was eleven and standing with others around a campfire, being brought to tears by my own story. For me, those tears were completely unexpected. I realized that during my week at camp, Jesus had taken me deeper in my relationship with him, but I didn't *really* realize it until I shared about when I first accepted Christ in Sunday school as an eight-year-old. I realized in that moment that I thought my prayer as an eight-year-old was simply so I didn't have to go to hell. But at eleven, I had actually met the living God as someone who wanted to be in relationship with me *right then*, not just at the end of my life on earth.

I have no idea what I actually said that night, but I was transformed spiritually by trying to share what God was doing inside me. After that tearful moment, I didn't share my story again for a long time, because I was so caught off-guard by the tears, and I felt like a fake Christian because of the first three years of my baby Christian life. I was afraid that I still didn't have it all figured out and that I would cry again.

As an adult, I realize that all of this was amazing spiritually and developmentally. I've struggled with pride my whole life, and I'm sure it's partly because I'm a middle child who felt like she always needed to look like she knew what she was doing. But now that I've been working with youth for so many years, I can see that it was normal for someone my age not to be able to understand the depths of Christ's desire to be in relationship with me, as I did when I was eleven. And of course I didn't know how to explain what God was doing inside me spiritually. Totally normal. Telling our stories helps us see God at work in our own lives and gives others the opportunity to hear what God is doing in other people's lives. We can learn even from ourselves if we're challenged to do things like share our spiritual stories.

More than twenty years ago, as a twenty-two-year-old youth director, I was invited to take the class, "How to Win Friends and Influence People" by Dale Carnegie. I believe I was the oldest person there. They were piloting something new, a class for "young adults" only, and they wanted graduates from high school all the way through college to take it. I had just finished my graduate work at Wheaton College, but they let me join anyway, as someone from our church was offering a scholarship so they could get a few more guinea pigs to test the course on a group of younger people.

They first taught us all about the elevator speech. Every week of class, everyone had to share a ninety-second story about anything to get us ready to win friends and influence people. When I heard that, I knew what God was calling me to do. He wanted me to win friends to him and to influence people toward following him. I decided in my heart that night that every ninety-second talk I gave in class would be about Jesus and what God was doing in my life.

I had just become a full-time youth director at a church, and I knew I needed to get better at talking about God in front of people. I needed to learn how to share Jesus in a dynamic way to one of the toughest audiences: teenagers. So every week I showed up at class with my ninety-second God story and shared it with a mostly non-Christian crowd. As I shared, I grew more confident in my speaking skills and in how God was working in my life. I ended up loving coming to that class twice a week, because I knew God was transforming me into the person he wanted me to be as I shared what he was doing in my life.

It was a powerful practice—so powerful that the closest person to my age in that class became a good friend. By the end of the summer, we were hanging out outside of class. And before long, right in my living room as we were chatting, she asked me about how to be in a relationship with Christ. She prayed that day in my house to receive Christ into her life. Then, on the last day of class, the class voted for me to win its one award. I was dumbfounded, because I thought people who love Jesus and talk about it are hated by the world.

That day my perspective changed. That day I learned that the world is hurting and broken, and people want to know Jesus. They *do* want to hear about the great things God can do. The award wasn't significant to me because I'd finally won a popularity contest at school but because I had done it by sharing what God was doing in my life.

Okay, so now you're like, please teach me to tell stories like that, right? It's really very simple. You stay focused on a set of questions and answer them so people can track with you—and most importantly, not get bored. Here are the questions: When did it happen? Where did it happen? Who was involved? Then, Dale Carnegie would say, what was the action you took? And what was the benefit you received?

Over the years, I've adapted the second half of the talk by adding, "What happened?" and "What was the action you took to follow God? What was the benefit you received from God?"

Here is my coming-to-Christ story in this format:

- *When did it happen?* When I was eight years old.
- *Where did it happen?* In Sunday school class in the basement of my church.
- *Who was involved?* Me, Mrs. Mellish (my Sunday school teacher), and God.

▓ *What happened?* Mrs. Mellish told me about Jesus dying on the cross for my sins and that if I was in relationship with him, I wouldn't go to hell, but I would get to live forever with Jesus in heaven.

▓ *What action did I take to follow God?* I prayed and asked Jesus to come into my heart so I wouldn't go to hell when I died.

▓ *What benefit did I receive from God?* I will live with Christ for eternity.

This format really does work with any story you want to tell. Give it a try. Pause for a moment to recall a God moment you've had recently, and see if you can fit it into this format.

One of the difficult pieces of the format is realizing you don't have to share as many details of the story as you may think. By limiting yourself to these questions, you actually leave your audience wanting more rather than being bored and wishing you would move on or stop talking. We all know those people— and some of us *are* those people.

As leaders, we tend to worry about having people share their stories in church or at events. When we ask them to share for two minutes, that often turns into a long, boring ten-minute story with details that just confuse people. I use the Carnegie technique when we train for the mission field, so we're all ready to share the hope that we have within us. I also use it when we have people sharing in church.

At first people thought that method would keep the Spirit from moving, but now we realize it frees up more people to share what God is doing in their lives, allowing the Spirit to be alive and well in worship on Sunday mornings rather than everything feeling dull. Our youth Sunday each year, during which both mentors and youth share, is one of the most favorite

Sundays of the year, with twenty-plus people sharing how God is on the move in their lives. However, if there were no boundaries on the talks, it would be the worst Sunday. Those twenty short stories become the sermon for the day, captivating all ages for the full hour.

Leading the Ninety-Second Testimony

Preparation

Print out the following questions with room to write answers. This usually fits on half a sheet of paper, which feels less overwhelming to most people than a full sheet.

- When did it happen?
- Where did it happen?
- Who was involved?
- What happened?
- What was the action you took with God?
- What was the spiritual benefit you received from God?

During

I explain the process of how to share their story, and I model it by telling my story. If you wanted to, read straight from this book to give them an idea of how it works.

I then give them a moment to think about the God story they want to practice sharing. Thirty seconds to a minute is a good amount of time, because you're going to take some time to walk through each question. They just need a story in general to start.

Then I call out the first question—When did it happen?—and encourage them to write down their answer. I give them only about fifteen seconds, because this process works only as it keeps the story concise. I then ask a few people to say when their story happened. It's good for the whole group to hear different ways to explain this in one sentence, such as, "I was eight years old," "The year was 1980 something," "Before church started." Sharing the *when* part of the story should start to build a mental picture of the story for the people listening. You want people to picture what happened so they feel like they were there.

I walk through each question with this same format so people have time to build their stories on paper as well as to start to verbalize them with the group.

After you've walked through the full set of questions, have them turn to a partner and share their story. When I do this, I set the timer for ninety seconds and say, "Ready, set, go." No matter what, after ninety seconds, I call out, "Switch," and make sure they switch, even if they haven't finished telling their stories.

After they've practiced one-on-one, I encourage them to tell their stories to everyone around their table. I ask each table to have someone keep time and to celebrate with anyone who keeps it to ninety seconds or less.

After

At the end of sharing, ask a few people to share with the whole group. I like to move from one-on-one to small groups to large groups, because when on mission trips, this is often what happens with personal stories of coming to faith.

As we prepare for our youth Sunday each year, I teach the mentors and students together and then encourage the mentors and the parents to help the youth be really ready for the ninety-second moment by practicing it and writing it out together. After I've taught and practiced this concept with the group as well as entrusted them to their parents and mentors, I let the adults know that if it doesn't end up in that exact format, it's fine, because the format is only to help everyone be able to share their story well.

Try to remember as a leader that this is a tool to be able to share God stories, not something that has to be so rigid that we don't give room for what God is doing. Hold this practice loosely after you've explained it well and walked through it well.

Debrief with the group at the end. You can ask, "What was hard about this practice?" or "What was fun about this practice?" or "How may you use this practice beyond what we're practicing for right now?"

One year, we used this spiritual practice at our high school ski retreat. When we first introduced it, the youth turned to one another during worship and shared their spiritual story with the person they were sitting next to. Then they wrote out their story in the prayer room on their own. Then it was written onto a ski tag attached to their ski jacket. On skiing day, they were encouraged to share their spiritual stories on the lifts.

I had a great time riding up with different kids each time, asking them to share their spiritual story with me. At the end of the weekend, we asked a few students to share what God had done in them over the weekend, using the same format. It was powerful to watch high school students share their stories. Find ways to use this practice when you'd really like people to share what God is doing in their lives.

YOUR LIFE SOUNDTRACK

Most people's lives are filled with music. A lot of us really enjoy it, so we create playlists on our phones that we can listen to easily and often. For this spiritual practice, you'll create a playlist that's like a soundtrack of your life, allowing you not only to explore your journey through life to better reflect on it but also to share your life with others. We then can share our spiritual stories through music.

I personally have zero musical talent or even abilities. If this is you too, please try this practice anyway, as it can be fun even for nonmusical people. Basically participants will make a soundtrack of their life that reflects their spiritual journey.

Leading Your Life Soundtrack

Instruct those in the group to draw a timeline of their life, marking as many spiritual moments as they can think of. I suggest about ten. I usually start with when I prayed to accept Christ. Some other ideas are baptism, a camp conversion, being called into ministry, or committing more fully to Christ. Let participants know they can put anything on their timeline that they see as a part of their spiritual story. When they make their soundtrack, it may or may not make the cut. This part of the process can take five to ten minutes, depending on the age of your group. Stay aware of your group's involvement as they're creating their timelines. If a person is stuck, have her share to help others come up with more markers on her timeline.

Give the group permission to open their phones to find songs that match up with their timeline markers. Before they do this, I usually share my soundtrack. My first song is "Great Balls of Fire," by Jerry Lee Lewis, because I came to Christ because I didn't want to go to hell. This is always good for a laugh as I share my story, making it more engaging. Songs that reflect the harder parts of my story give me space for me to jump in the deep end faster, if I think it's a good place to share about the highs and lows of my spiritual story in a short time. When I share my spiritual soundtrack with a larger group, I sometimes play a few seconds of each song before sharing my story. Each song pops in for just a moment to draw everyone into my story.

This way of sharing works especially well with teenagers, because they enjoy sharing their music with peers. And they have earbuds, so they can share with just one other person. I've also used it in prayer rooms with all ages, giving people plenty of time to create their playlists.

Part of this lengthy process is figuring out the latest technology and where or how your participants will create their playlists. If the technology piece is getting in the way of progress, encourage people simply to write out their playlist. They can create an electronic playlist later if they'd like. If it's an intergenerational group, give the younger generation an opportunity to pair up with someone who's struggling. Remember that the whole reason for gathering to do spiritual practices is to build a relationship not only with God but also with others.

LISTENING GROUPS

I love this spiritual practice because one of the biggest losses we're experiencing as a result of social media and the modern conveniences of email and texting is the loss of physical presence with one another. As a pastor, I often find myself feeling like I'm entering into a fresh new conversation on social media—but I haven't, because other people have posted the first parts of the conversation, which I may or may not have read. I've also found myself trying to enter into a conversation with someone and am cut off with a statement like, "All of this is on Facebook. You read that, right?" I had read it, but I was hoping to give that person the time, the space, and the gift of listening to her heart in an actual face-to-face moment.

I've always valued relationships and people above anything else, so reading something on social media causes me to want more. I long for others to desire deep intimacy with others. Part of this desire is my background in psychology. I know people need to process things verbally face to face, and having people listen and engage can be very healing to a soul.

Listening groups (also called group spiritual direction) are very effective in this. I use listening groups in multiple settings for two main reasons: to give individuals space to grow, learn, and process their individual spiritual lives, and to bond people in deep personal ways in spiritual community.

I have used this spiritual practice with groups as small as three and as large as two hundred, such as when I invited our church's Board of Spiritual Life to engage in it when we were at a two-day retreat together. It was our first evening there. We'd had dinner and had engaged in one group session with a guest speaker. In one room were the church staff, a few spouses of staff, and our Board of Spiritual Life. The group consisted of government workers, retired businessmen, young adults in their first jobs, and everyone in-between.

As we came out of that session, I started to doubt that we should do the touchy-feely, go-to-the-depths-of-your-soul activity I'd planned. I figured I was about to get a lot of eye rolling and questions. Almost every time I'm about to lead this practice, I start to doubt. This is a part of the process.

My new boss looked at me, and I knew it was time to start, but I sure didn't want to lead in that moment. But being a dutiful person, I went for it. Within minutes, people in the room were sharing their spiritual stories deeper than I'd ever heard them share in the five years I'd known them. I was captivated as I watched businessmen tear up and share mighty things God was doing in their lives. People were connecting God's grace from twenty years before to why they still served in a church. I was thankful in that moment that I'd stuck with God's plan to move forward and lead rather than recoil and lean on my own understanding.

I must also say I tried to lead this same spiritual practice with high school students, and it may be the worst Sunday school class ever in the history of my church. The youth looked at me and asked, "Why are you making us do this?" So it doesn't always work, but it's worth a try.

Leading a Listening Group

Get ready

Encourage participants to gather in groups of three with people they'd like to share with at a deep level. Have them create a mini triangle, facing each other so they can make good eye contact. Also encourage them to create as much distance from the other groups as they can, so it's easier to hear each another without distraction. They may need to move around the room to do this, so give time and space for it.

Tell them that each person in the group will have a chance to share, and ask them all to listen without giving input. Tell them they'll have time to respond to one another and that you'll guide them through each part of the process of sharing and listening. Also remind them to keep what's said in the group confidential.

Encourage everyone in the room to close their eyes for one minute to prepare for what God wants them to process with the group. Usually something comes to participants' minds right away. Other times, the group needs a prompt. This can be a general or a more specific prompt. I encourage people to share about something in their lives that feels complicated or hard. You can use other prompts, particularly if the participants are in a teaching session. For example, if teaching on evangelism, use prompts like, "Share when you've been successful—or unsuccessful—in sharing your faith. Or talk about someone you'd like to share your faith with, but you aren't sure how you would do it." Any prompt is fine; the goal is to give people permission to share deeply and to give space for others to speak into their lives.

During the practice

Start the time by praying. Aloud, ask God to speak to each person in a moment of silence as to what he wants them to process. Fall silent for one full minute. (Use your timer.) You may be tempted to go longer or shorter than a minute, but it's important to stay on time for this whole practice. If you don't, it will take too long. At the end of the one minute of silence, simply say amen.

Hopefully at least one person in each of the triads has heard something God is asking them to process. Tell the participants to decide which person will share first, or I say, "Raise your hand if you're going first." Or count down from five to help them decide quickly. Tell them this person will share uninterrupted for three minutes about what's going on in his or her life; the other two people will listen. Add that the important part of the practice is holding the space well and that you will explain that part as they go.

If you feel it would be good for the group, encourage them to take the risk of going deeper than usual so everyone feels permission to go deep as they share. Then say, "Ready, set, go." Set your timer for three minutes. As time dwindles, give time warnings at one minute, thirty seconds, and especially ten seconds.

During these three minutes, the other members of the group listen without interjecting, make good eye contact, nod their heads, and make uh-huh noises. Instruct them that if the person finishes before the whole group moves on, they should prayerfully stay silent and attentive as they reflect on what they've heard. Some people need silence before they say more. And some feel more respected when people don't try to fill the silence. People find this practice powerful because they rarely experience such listening.

After the first person has shared for the full three minutes, encourage the group to take one minute to ask the first speaker clarifying questions only. Give examples to the group, such as, "You said the name Bob. Is Bob your husband or your uncle?" Clarifying questions are for when you don't understand something or you missed an important detail. Don't try to draw out more of the story. Don't ask questions just out of curiosity.

After the clarifying questions have been asked and answered in one minute or less, ask the group to fall silent for one minute. Saying something like, "During the next minute, you are waiting for a word, phrase, or image to come to mind as a result of what you've heard your group member say." Set your timer for one minute.

At the end of the minute, say amen and encourage the listeners to tell the sharer the word, phrase, or image that came to mind. Tell them that as they share the word, phrase, or image, they aren't to explain to the sharer what they think it means. They're simply to say the word, phrase, or image that came to mind.

After this has been said, the sharer has the opportunity to respond by simply saying thank you, by writing them down to process later, or by responding to the two people individually or together.

Often participants take the moment to say how the word, phrase, or image sits with them in that moment. Give the group about three minutes to respond to each other. If there is time, listeners can share things they noticed in the sharer, such as, "I noticed when you talked about your brother, you teared up." Remind participants to make sure they aren't telling the sharer what it means but just mentioning what they saw so the sharer can process it with God.

After

To close this time, encourage the group to fall into silent prayer for the person who shared. Verbalize that if participants want there to be a growing edge or community-building moment, they need to give space not only to pray for the sharer but also to give space for the next person to share.

Start the whole process again with the next person presenting. If you don't hold true to the time frames, this process can get very long. Stay on task continually so all people in the group get their full time. Even with groups of three, this process takes about forty-five minutes, which will fly by. It's very easy for this process to end up being an hour if you don't keep it moving.

After everyone in the group has had time to share and receive, debrief to make sure confidentiality is upheld and that participants can feel good about what they shared and not too vulnerable as they leave the space. While still in groups, have the three participants share what they found helpful. Also have them share what was hard to share in their group. Then have them share a few words of encouragement.

Note that encouragement is different from advice. Encouragement is pointing out something a person did well; advice is telling people what they should do. If you hear people giving advice, say to the whole group, "Make sure you are only encouraging people, not giving advice."

Finally, say to the group, "What we've just shared in this group is confidential. Do not share this information outside this group. If people who shared want to continue talking about their story outside this group, they are welcome to do so, but the listeners are to reengage with someone else's story only if they're invited into that conversation by the person who shared."

Also add, "If you feel vulnerable, that's very normal. Feel free to let your group know how important it is for you that they not share outside the group. If someone breaks this confidence, it's okay to confront that person and to let the leader know that the confidence was broken. On the flipside, if you enjoyed sharing what you did, continue sharing with your group and others as well."

Close with a word of prayer for the group.

THE RHYTHM *of* LIFE *in* COMMUNITY

As I was finishing my seminary work, I was also dating my husband-to-be. I worked full time as a youth pastor, and our senior pastor was just about to go on a leave of absence. My life rhythm was in chaos. And as God would have it, I had committed to go to a retreat to teach a group of leaders about how to find their life rhythm.

I remember racing over to my parents' house for my father's birthday, with my boyfriend in tow. We then gave my dad a day of work in his yard. I had stayed up way too late the night before, desperately trying to do an extra-credit assignment for a class I wasn't doing the best in. Sweaty, tired, and gross, I raced back home to drop off my boyfriend, pack, and race to the retreat. I said goodbye to my boyfriend instead of taking a shower, and off I went for a twenty-four-hour retreat. I fought hard not to fall asleep at the wheel on the two-hour drive there. Then I raced in the meeting room with seconds to spare and ironically taught people how to create a healthy life rhythm.

THE SPIRITUAL AND BIBLICAL PERSPECTIVE ON LIFE RHYTHM

As Christ walked the earth, he had a life rhythm. He took time to pull away from the crowd and spend time with the Father. "Very early in the morning, while it was still dark, Jesus got up, left the house and went off to a solitary place, where he prayed" (Mark 1:35). This took place right after he healed many with various diseases and drove out demons.

Jesus knew what he needed to do to have a healthy rhythm in ministry. He needed to get away to a solitary place to pray, "early in the morning, while it was still dark" (Mark 1:35). Crowds of people came to hear him and to be healed of their sicknesses. "But Jesus often withdrew to lonely places and prayed" (Luke 5:16). The word *often* is key here. Jesus had a life rhythm, and he kept it even in the midst of crowds coming to him to be healed.

If Jesus needed to do this, we need it all the more. We need to find ways to get away from doing ministry to meet with the living God. This chapter provides a way to take all you've learned, practiced, and processed in the book so far and integrate it into real life. This will help you and the people you lead in this practice to see what draws you close to the heart of God and what doesn't. This chapter will give you the space to work out a way of life that's transformational over the long haul. My hope is that these last four spiritual practices help you find the spiritual rhythm within you and your community.

SABBATH

"Since the promise of entering [God's] rest still stands, let us be careful that none of you be found to have fallen short of it"

(Hebrews 4:1). In the past six years, I've seen an increase in the number of teens and their parents being diagnosed with anxiety disorders. Most people can relate to having high-anxiety moments, but this standard way of feeling in a large sector of our community is new. In the past six years, as I have been watching teens, college students, and young adults do life, I've noticed more and more of them experiencing more stress and anxiety than ever before.

"What do you want to do when you grow up?" used to be a fun question for students to answer. Now it has the opposite effect. It's one more high-pressure question coming at them. It's the same with the question, "Do you know where you'll be going to college?"

When I first started ministry, I heard phrases like, "I can't wait to grow up and be an adult!" and "I can't wait to drive so I can go wherever I want to go," and "I can't wait to have my own place." I almost never hear them anymore. Eight years ago, for the first time, I heard an eighteen-year-old express no desire to get a driver's license or to ever drive. Then I heard it more and more. Students wish they were kids again and say they don't want to grow up. They want to live with their parents after college.

My head can hardly take it in. And I wonder what's happening in the lives of youth today that wasn't ten years ago. For one, they have zero empty space in their lives. We're all living at a frantic pace every day. Families are running from one practice to another without a break to catch our breath or even to eat a meal. Young people are trying to do it all while trying to keep a 4.0-plus grade point average so they get good scholarships for college. And parents are making it happen—or at least cheering it on at close range.

When young people find themselves in stillness or quiet, they activate their brains as quickly as possible by picking up their phones. They don't know how to be still and know he is God. They become fearful in the void of activity and forward movement. They're constantly under pressure to accomplish great things and to be productive. This is why I think mindless social media is so appealing. When they scroll, they're seeking places that don't require purpose and accomplishment.

A sabbath gives space for the restoration needed to combat anxiety and life's pressures. And doing sabbath corporately is important. Actually, keeping it works only if you do it corporately in some shape or form. If you're trying to do it as an individual, you're likely to fail. No matter who you are, if you want to reserve a day for sabbath, you have to do it within your community context. That likely means your family, your place of work, and those closest to you.

Since I work on Sundays, I tell my congregation what my day off is. Otherwise, they don't know what day to expect no return calls from me, no texts, no reply to emails. If they know, I'm more likely to be able to keep a sabbath and my job as a pastor.

I may have lost you already, because you're thinking, *This lady does not get it. We no longer live in a world where this is even remotely possible, let alone something I want to do. Stop working for twenty-four hours? Yeah, right.*

I get it. I live in this world too. Almost no one stops for a full twenty-four hours—even on Thanksgiving and Christmas, let alone one day a week, every week. I would love to say I take twenty-four hours every week to shut down my life just like everyone did in biblical times. But the reality is, I do not—but I *try* weekly. It has taken the past two thousand years to get far away from the concept of sabbath, so I know it will take you and your community many weeks, months, and even years to gain it back.

Pause for a moment right now. What do you long for? How much would you enjoy a day of true sabbath?

I know a family that stops using all electronic devices every Sunday afternoon in order to move themselves in the direction of experiencing sabbath life together. I love this idea, and it reminds me of a concept in the Jewish tradition called the Sabbath box. A Sabbath box is found in some Jewish households, and it holds anything that isn't needed or shouldn't be used during the Sabbath, such as pens, keys, and wallets. They put anything in the box that may distract them from loving God and loving those who are in the room with them. Today the box includes cell phones, tablets, and laptops. Most televisions wouldn't fit in such a box, but you get the idea.

A few years ago, when I first heard about this concept, I loved it so much I found a large shoebox and collaged it with magazine pictures that reminded me of how I wanted to spend my time. I then cut very strategic holes in the box to make it a charging station for our two cell phones and our two iPads. For a season, each night when I came home from work, I put my devices into the box and plugged them in. As I did this, I said to myself and to my husband, "I am not working any more tonight." So instead of coming through the door and losing my whole evening texting, working, and ignoring my husband, I became a present spouse who engaged fully with life at home.

Then we used the box one day to catch a mouse, and it went in the trash. I think it's time for me to make a new box—maybe slightly bigger so it can charge my laptop too, since it has been a year of writing a book after work and on my days off.

If you want sabbath enough and seek after it weekly, you can catch glimpses of rest and restoration together. Some weeks you'll fall short, but not trying at all in our current culture will guarantee that you have no sabbath in your life at all—or even a sliver of emotional or spiritual rest. Reclaim your life with Christ!

Someone once told me she turned off her phone once a day for one hour to have a piece of sabbath rest. She did it when she got the most activity on her phone. It was her way of taking back a big part of her day that was getting lost.

Doing a one-hour spiritual practice each morning during Lent can protect your morning devotion time with God. For me, that one hour a day shifted the addictive relationship I had with my phone. The morning stillness had always triggered thoughts about who I needed to be connecting with and what I needed to get done at work. Before I even noticed, I'd lost a significant amount of my time with God. Those things weren't bad, especially because my job is ministry, but they distracted me during what was supposed to be my focused time alone with God.

My favorite time of day was getting swallowed up by my poor phone habits and lack of boundaries, yet I was giving it away without even noticing. If you find yourself thinking, *I'm not addicted to my phone,* I challenge you to turn it off while you read the rest of this book. If that idea raises anxiety in your soul, you may have an addiction. If you can't bring yourself to turn it off right now, you definitely have an addiction. I challenge you to put your phone on airplane mode for just one minute. After one minute, assess how you're feeling. Keep trying to increase the amount of time you're disconnected from your phone as a way of seeking healing.

Some of these ideas mean being device-free for one hour, three hours, or even a full twenty-four hours. But start with baby steps. If you're anything like me, as you read these last few paragraphs, you found yourself longing to be detached from devices and other things. You also realized you can make adjustments if you decide to, but it will never happen if you don't act.

If you were to add two of these changes in a week, you could have eleven or twelve hours of sabbath in a week. That way, you won't feel you have to quit all your activities and even your job to gain sabbath. Then you're only thirteen hours away from a twenty-four-hour sabbath in a week, and most of that can be sleeping hours. I'm sure there are hundreds of ways we could move ourselves back to twenty-four hours of sabbath rest each week.

Here's an important question to ask ourselves: What are we gaining by never stopping? I know I gain negative things when I ignore sabbath—even when I fill my life with positive things the entire time. How is this possible? Maybe two negatives make a positive. Negative time on my phone plus negative time working equals a positive attitude and positive relationships with God and others. Strange how working my job for only the hours I'm supposed to can make me better at my job.

If we follow God's equation for how life works in Scripture, we should expect life to work. After all, he is the "pioneer and perfecter of faith" (Hebrews 12:2). He knows how our lives work best. I realize that taking an hour here and there during the week to add up to a full twenty-four hours isn't a "true" sabbath. But such steps will whet your appetite for the full twenty-four hours, and you'll work toward that goal by starting with smaller practices. Again, if you and your community are all working toward this goal together, it will be far more achievable.

One of the things that caused me to long for sabbath in my life was learning about all the things Jews are allowed to do during the Sabbath. Things that are offered are things I love to do: Spend time with friends and family. Take naps. Eat together.

Relax. Talk. Be still. Engage with God. Spend time in nature. If you don't know much about sabbath, I encourage you to find a book on it and enjoy reading about how to rest. It is a lost art.

Leading Sabbath

Before

Start practicing sabbath yourself in some way. On most of my Thursday afternoons at work, I have a moment that looks much like the scene from *Fiddler on the Roof* when the whole family is frantically preparing for the Sabbath. I work fast, doing more in a short time in an effort to do less on Fridays. I rarely fully experience sabbath, but I'm always thankful for the little taste of sabbath I get when I'm able to do moments of it well.

Try at least one personal step toward sabbath before you lead others in this practice. Or be upfront with the group you're leading; tell them you want to try to do it with them. Then lead your group in a discussion that will help them decide how you're all going to live out sabbath together. Learn what challenges they're willing to tackle. Brainstorm ideas together.

During

Once you've laid out the plan for your sabbath, decide how you're actually going to pull it off together. Discuss creative ways to engage, write down specific activities, mark goals on your calendars, and encourage each other. Learn about having a rhythm of life or a rule of life. Read Wayne Muller's *Sabbath* together to get lots of ideas for living into sabbath as a community.

After

After you've decided as a group how you'll live into your sabbath, discuss ways to check with one another to encourage one another when there's progress and to pray for one another when it doesn't seem to be working. If you're doing this as a church, during worship on Sundays, invite people to share how they were able to pull it off that week or even ways they failed that reminded them they wanted to try again next week. Keeping the concept of sabbath in front of people regularly will help you be successful as a community.

Pray for each other, asking God to be the God of your sabbath and to give you the courage to stop in life.

PERSONAL SANCTUARY

I was first introduced to the concept of personal sanctuary by Hellen Cepero in one of my spiritual direction classes more than ten years ago. She encouraged us to take paper and crayons outside and draw ten things that helped us connect with God. I was thirty-something at the time and one of the youngest people in the class. I felt fully alive as I went outside, sat in the grass, and began to draw. I'm sure some of my classmates wondered why they were being asked to use crayons in a seminary-level class.

For the first time in my life, I named ten things I loved to do to experience the presence of God. As I drew, I realized I didn't think about this often. I also realized that sometimes my time with God had been out of obligation, not out of genuine desire to be near him. This process helped me let go of some "shoulds" I'd connected to my spiritual life. It gave me a chance to see ways I loved to connect with God and opened several new ways I hadn't considered. It gave me permission to experience God in a more joy-filled way.

I drew things like a candle, coffee, walking outside, listening to worship music, meeting one-on-one with people, reading, and journaling. I had never considered lighting a candle each time I sat down in the morning to meet with God. In my head, candles were for special occasions. Somehow I thought it would take more effort to light a candle than it does. A candle made my time with God feel more sacred, important, and intimate.

So taking those fifteen minutes to draw what I loved opened up a new reality. It wouldn't have happened if I hadn't been given permission.

Now I sit daily in my same chair with my puppies. I eat my breakfast and sip my coffee. I sometimes light a candle. All these small things engage me. I feel ready to read and write in the presence of God. When I take the time to do this each day, I feel ready and centered for my day. I feel encouraged and inspired to be the person God is calling me to be that day. This space makes me feel refreshed and renewed.

Yet I know that for someone else, sitting is the worst way to connect with God. So when you think about your own personal sanctuary, the most important thing to consider is how you connect best with God. For example, one of my coworkers' favorite ways to connect with God is to walk and pray.

Help ministry leaders remember how important it is for them to take time to be with the living God. Each of us is wired differently, so each of us needs to discover how we best connect with God along the way. Each time I lead this exercise with others, I redraw my personal sanctuary.

Over the years, I've also realized my sanctuary is different from season to season. I love to be in the sun or near water, to walk or jog outside. But I live in the Chicago area, so I can be outside in the sun only about six months of the year. Therefore, I need to change my personal sanctuary seasonally. If I redo it in the late fall and in the early spring, I have much better success overall with my time with God.

You'll find out how to lead the creation of a personal sanctuary after the following section on life rhythm, because they work together.

FINDING A LIFE RHYTHM

Creating a personal sanctuary has helped me to be able to think about my *rule* of life as a *rhythm* of life. A rule of life is something we have so God rules our lives instead of our lives ruling us. Stephen Macchia and Mark Buchanan's book *Crafting a Rule of Life: An Invitation to a Well-Ordered Way* can help you go deeper. Also visit Macchia's website, "Crafting a Rule of Life," to see how people have created very different rules to make them life-giving for themselves. *Sacred Rhythms* by Ruth Haley Barton can lead you through a way to create a rhythm of life as well.

When creating a rule of life for yourself, think about how you do life daily, weekly, monthly, and yearly. When I started to think about life this way, I realized I could experience life differently. I realized I didn't have to be tossed to and fro by whatever came across my path on any given day. I had the option to choose how I wanted to engage with God.

Doing this assessment freed me to live according to the rhythm God has for me rather than according to whatever people bring to me on any given day. I realized I could be proactive. For example, God showed me that I love spending time with him each morning over breakfast. I no longer had to let the rest of my day dictate if I had time for this or not. No matter what, I could always wake up early enough to give myself this rhythm. God also let me know that most of the world has a full two-day weekend and that I could have the same if I guarded those days as he was calling me to do.

Most pastors are expected to be fully committed, which I am—and I love it. However, I was learning that if I didn't have time off, away from the duties of the church, I wasn't the pastor God was calling me to be. Realizing how important it was for me to take a sabbath day every week and a normal Saturday like everyone else in the world was very important. In the past six years, I've become very aware that most people in the world aren't taking a real sabbath or any sort of downtime. We're living in a world that's constantly forcing people to be on the go. If we have downtime, we are on some sort of technical device, often causing us to be more on than off.

When trying to create a rhythm of life for your family, have your whole family draw a picture with ten ways they engage with God—for kids you can say, "What are ten ways you can feel Jesus?" After everyone has taken ten minutes or so to draw these pictures, talk about them as a family. Notice if there is anything that all your pictures have in common, like prayer together before dinner or reading a Bible story before bed or going to church together or taking family walks. Find that one way that you all have in common, and make sure it's a part of your family rhythm.

Leading Personal Sanctuary and Finding a Life Rhythm

Preparation

You'll need one piece of paper per person, and colored pencils, thin markers, or crayons so everyone has a few colors each. Multiple colors unlock the creative side of our brains. If nothing else, choose colored pencils, since they work best for all ages.

Creating a sanctuary

When everyone has both paper and writing utensils, ask them to work right where they are in the room, or give them permission to create some of their own space to meet silently with God. Tell them, "As you're alone with God for the next fifteen minutes, try to draw ten ways you connect best with him. These are ways you create your own sanctuary." Ask the group to draw only on one side of the paper. Also remind them that God can translate pictures that no one else may understand, so they shouldn't worry how good the drawing is. They can get in touch with God by drawing however they wish.

If you keep everyone in the room, every five minutes ask a few people to share something they've added to their sanctuary to help other people think of more ideas for themselves.

After about fifteen minutes of giving participants time to draw and meet with God, have them share with the group what they drew. Give them permission to add to their drawing as they're listening, especially if they hear something from someone else that they know would be good for them as well.

Once you feel enough people have had space to share, ask specifically if anyone drew any of the spiritual practices you taught them. Give an opportunity to name some practices they didn't draw. Encourage them to add them if they know they would enjoy doing them more often.

Finding a life rhythm

After they're done drawing additional practices, ask them to fold their drawing into quarters, folding the paper in half and then in half again.

Give them instructions like the following: "In one of the quadrants, write the word *daily*. In that quadrant write what you can do in your sanctuary every day or at least four or five days a week—for example, read my Bible, pray, or journal." Give the group a moment to flip the paper over to look at what they drew earlier to find the ways they can connect with God daily.

After about two minutes, have them share some of the ways they can connect with God daily. Again, sharing can help others in the group get more ideas.

Tell them to write the word *weekly* in the next quadrant. Again give them time to flip back and forth to transfer what they drew into the section labeled *weekly*. Help them find just one or two things they think they could pull off once a week to connect with God.

Tell them to write *monthly* in the next quadrant. At this point, help participants understand why they'd put something in the monthly spot rather than the weekly spot. For example, few of us have time every week to meet a friend for coffee, do an art project, and go to spiritual direction. However, we can pull them all off comfortably each month.

As before, give participants time to pick one or two things they could do to connect with God monthly. This should be something that takes more for them to pull off, like meeting with a friend or doing a woodworking project. Encourage the group to share some of their ideas.

The final quadrant can be labeled *yearly* or *twice a year*. A good example for this section is a spiritual retreat, a Christian conference, or a relaxing vacation.

Tell the participants something like this: "After you have each quadrant filled in, circle one thing in each quadrant you're going to try tomorrow, this week, this month, and this year. Narrowing down what you try first will help you not feel like a failure if you didn't do it in your first week. This process is much like starting a new exercise regimen. If you work out too hard the first day or week, you'll be too sore to keep it up."

As I teach this process, I try to help people see and understand that a life rhythm helps them connect with God in a way that works for them. Though it's healthy for the individual, at the same time it must work for the family and the greater community.

One time a pastor and his wife, who was the children's pastor, were planning a family retreat, and he wanted to have each person come up with a life rhythm while they were there. The first response from his wife was, "No way will the process work."

I got pulled into the middle of the discussion. And I laughed as I was invited to talk to those two parents on speakerphone to help align their family again so they could finish planning the family retreat. As we began to talk, we journeyed our way through to a place we could all agree on: all the family members could draw a personal sanctuary. The younger they were, the harder the concept would be, but at least there could be coloring while the rest of the family worked to connect with God.

Then the real negotiating began. I first suggested that each family member pick one way they wanted to connect with God for each section. The wife chimed in right away: "This would stress me out, because we have four kids, and now I'm trying to get the family to do six new spiritual things. This doesn't feel life-giving to me."

I thought for a moment and said, "Do you think that after they have drawn their spiritual sanctuary, the whole family could share their pictures with one another and find one thing that all the pictures have in common? That could be the family's new spiritual rhythm that they do together."

She said, "Yes, that feels life-giving. That I could do. That we could do as a family."

And this is exactly what I want to leave you with as you finish this reading and implement this book: make sure everything you teach more than once is life-giving for you as the leader and for your group. My hope and prayer for you, as you let this book come alive in your ministry, is that it makes you and those you lead more fully alive in Christ. Amen!

9

CORPORATE
DISCERNMENT

DURING MY FIRST FEW YEARS OF MINISTRY, I grew tired of students and their parents telling me where they wanted to go on mission trips. It wasn't because of where they picked or because they wanted to be invested in the decision. After all, most pastors get excited when people get excited about missions. The problem was that students and parents weren't choosing a ministry location for the ministry. They were picking cool, exotic locations where they hadn't vacationed yet. In my frustration, I started using a discernment process to help them ask God where we should go, rather than just go to a place they wanted to check off their bucket list.

After years of using this process for mission trips, I realized it could be a discernment tool for just about anything. One time I asked an executive board of our church to use colored pencils to draw pictures during part of a board meeting as we asked God if we should do the building project we thought was a good idea. During that short time, God revealed far more godly reasons for us to renovate our building than we ever would have thought of in a traditional planning session. Instead of thinking of ways to sell the church on doing a building project, we found out who God wanted us to minister to through a newly renovated building and why he would have us do it at that time.

A simple discernment process takes the power players out of the power seat and gives the power back to God, where it belongs. Money is no longer the focus when asking God, "Should we build or not?" God may say something about money when you get to the last question, but prior to that, all the questions are focused on the mission and ministry that the church building will contain, not on whether the church can afford it. I'm reminded over and over that if God wants something to happen, he makes it happen. He makes a way where there seems to be no way. Of course, God also gives us the freedom of choice, so even with the hard work of seeking discernment, group members may not all arrive on the same page.

In this process, we ask God simple questions we sometimes forget to ask before we make our move. This means taking the time to listen for how God answers rather than answering as we normally would. The problem with this process is we're humans, so we hear what we want to hear, even if it isn't from God. We filter every thought through our own personal biases. We let the process confirm what we already believe and want. This is normal. As you engage in the process, know this will happen, and do your best to push toward God's mindset, not your own.

In corporate discernment, we ask God the questions we often forget to ask when we need to make big decisions. We seek God about something specific. This process is not fail-safe, of course, but it's one way to get in the mode of discerning what God may be saying. It gives you a new way to ask God for help in making a big decision, but it doesn't guarantee you've heard the voice of God.

This process can bring clarity but also can lead to more questions—and even confusion. As you allow yourself to pray over specific questions, you may hear specific answers that are just you thinking what you want. Try not to see this process as the end all and be all of your discernment process, but one step in the many steps toward what God may be trying to do in and through you.

It's impossible to have perfect communication with God; our humanness gets in the way. We all want to go on that cool vacation of a lifetime, so our minds fixate on that, not on hearing something new God could say. This is human. But we still hear from God in and among our desires. See if you can discern which is which and where there is overlap so you can move toward God's calling. This is a part of being human.

God wants to speak. The question is, do we want to hear what he has to say? Better to have asked God and only hear half of what he has to say than not to ask and hear nothing.

THE WHO, WHAT, WHEN, WHERE, WHY, AND HOW OF DISCERNMENT

Before you lead this process, do it yourself first.

Find a quiet place and forty minutes to an hour so you can be patient and hear the still small voice of God. I start by folding a large sheet of paper in fourths. This can also be done in a journal with a pen or even using technology. (However, when I use technology, I tend to forget to listen for the voice of God. I go into full-blown planning mode, including surfing the internet to do research. I'm always one click away from disconnecting from

God.) Work hard to still your work-mode mindset, and listen for the voice of God.

You will be drawing pictures and then writing. When we draw, we open up the creative side of ourselves. Also note that God often speaks in images, single words, or short phrases when we're still and listening. I think this is for our benefit, not his. If we were to hear all God has to say to us in one sitting, it would be overwhelming. In fact, reading the whole Bible takes most people at least a year, so in reality he doesn't tell us everything all at once. He gives us what we need when we need it. He's just waiting for us to ask and listen.

Put your paper and writing utensils out in front of you. Sit comfortably in your chair. Take a few deep breaths in and out. Then take a few moments to imagine yourself in the presence of God. Let yourself feel his presence for a minute or two. Ask God to speak and to silence anything else that may not be from him.

While you're in this spiritual space, state what you'd like to know. Say it out loud if you're alone. Simply hold the question in your mind and heart, or write it out. I find it most helpful to write out the question, so when I read it later in life, I can see if there was a direct way God answered my question. God does speak but not always in the way we want him to speak or when we ask him to speak. Your question is simply a way for you to be able to hear him whenever and however he speaks.

Proceed by asking God a series of six questions directly related to what you want to know his will on: Who? What? When? Where? Why? How?

In the upper corner in the first block on the paper, write, "Who?" Ask, "Lord, who are you asking me to minister to?" or "Who am I called to minister with on this mission trip?" or whatever is applicable. Give yourself at least three to five minutes to sit with this question. Close your eyes. Let images and words come to mind. As they do, draw them. As words or phrases come to mind, write them as freely as possible. Try not to block any thoughts, and don't worry about spelling or grammar. Free-write or draw anything that comes to mind, especially any Scripture.

If you get scared or overwhelmed by what you hear, remember this is God speaking, and he is more than able to do beyond what we can ask or imagine (Ephesians 3:20). You may think, *I could never do this*. That's correct, so remember this truth as you go through the process: "I can do all this through him who gives me strength" (Philippians 4:13). He never asks us to do things on our own or in our own power. If it becomes overwhelming, then you know God needs to move for it to happen.

Sometimes tears flow during this process. If this happens, pay attention. Try your best not to block God; remember, he's on the throne and is the King of kings and the Lord of lords. As the information stops or no longer flows out of you, write or say out loud, "Amen." Then move to the next block on your paper.

In the second space, write, "What?" in the corner of the block. Then ask God, "What are you calling me to do, Lord?" or "What am I called and gifted to do?" As you ask this question, let the Holy Spirit move in your heart. Remember that if tears flow, pay attention. This is one way the Holy Spirit expresses himself.

In the next block on your paper, write, "When?" As you start to draw and journal in this block, ask God, "When are you asking me to take the next step? When are you calling me to make things happen?" Let God speak. Listen. This is a good time to pull out a calendar and notice dates, seasons, and times of the year. In this block, try drawing a timeline, a season, or a calendar. Let yourself think about how the weather feels. This can be another way to hear the voice of God.

Write "Where" on your paper, and ask God, "Where are you calling me to go?" or "Where do I need to place myself to be fully able to answer your call on my life?" It may seem strange that I'm asking you to wait this long to ask the question, especially in relation to the mission trip example. As you listen for the voice of God, let your mind hear sounds that may help you know where you are to go. Let your mind see the vegetation of the land where you sense God is calling you. Draw buildings you see, and write down everything that comes to mind.

Once when doing this process in the suburbs, as a group discerning where to go on a mission trip, we heard the clip-clop of horse hoofs as we were deciding whether we should go to a rural, suburban, or urban area. I ran outside to see how God had spoken to us so clearly. There it was, a romantic holiday carriage ride—just when we needed it, of course.

Now write, "Why?" Most leaders encourage you to consider the why first, and we often think we know why at the beginning. However, as you move through this process, your answer to "Why?" may be deeper than it would have been at the beginning of this process. Ask God, "Why are you calling me to this ministry at this time?"

We usually start with this question when planning a mission trip or ministry event. But if you've gone about this process right, God has told you what he wants of you, so now you can ask God, "How?" "How do you want me to pull this off, Lord?"

BRING IT TOGETHER

After God has given you answers to these six questions, take a moment to go back through the six blocks and notice themes written in more than one block. As you find them, circle them and then write them in the seventh block. Label this block, "Themes." Also list in this block any Scriptures that have come to mind.

When working with a group, have participants name some of the themes that came up in their process. As someone names a theme, I ask the group if that same theme came up for anyone else. I list those on a board or large piece of paper that everyone can see. This allows the group to see and hear common themes and is useful for both small or large groups. This is the beauty of the Holy Spirit speaking; he doesn't aim to confuse but to clarify. Often the more people you have listening, the more clearly the Holy Spirit speaks. This is not brainstorming to get the most ideas; it is a powerful moment when the group hears the same thing being said by one person after another.

TEST WHAT YOU THINK YOU HEARD FROM GOD

In the last block on your paper, in your journal, or as you type, ask yourself these six questions to see if what you've heard is from God or from your own desires. (The following is adapted from Clint Bokelman's *Missions 101 Training Manual*.)

- Does what you have heard from God honor God?
- Does Scripture back up what you have heard?
- Do other Christians confirm what you've heard from God? (When I do this process with a group, I look for common themes running through what people have heard from God separately.)
- Will it produce good fruit?
- Have you lived into it to see if God makes it happen? When what I heard is not exactly what God is calling me to, it still points me in a better direction.

The reality is, if you're seeking God's will, you're usually choosing among two or more godly things. Therefore, you need to remind yourself that you may be more drawn to one than another. You're seeking discernment not so God will agree with you but so you come to agree with God. If you find yourself resisting, pay attention to that feeling, and ask yourself what your resistance is about. Are you resisting something because you're aware it's where God may want you to go?

When you find yourself resisting, engage in conversations with other believers. Consider creating a listening group or clearness committee, as described in chapter seven. These will help you talk out what God may be moving you toward or away from. In the end, discerning God's voice will always be subjective, but we can engage deeply in trying to discern God's call rather than just jumping in and seeing what happens.

Once you've taken yourself through this process, think about those you lead. What group of people needs to do this process with you? Is your congregation considering a building campaign? Is your board trying to decide what part of the strategic plan you should focus on? Are your small group leaders choosing the next Bible studies? Maybe your family needs to make a hard decision, such as whether you should move? Or maybe right in the middle of a mission trip you're trying to decide what your group needs to do the next day.

I've seen this process fail only when the people involved aren't invested prayerfully. It's also important for everyone to gain a buy-in before you start. It's okay if people are skeptical, but it's very important that they commit to the process, ask God to speak, and respond by actually trying to hear the voice of God. If people don't want to hear God's voice, then sure enough, they don't hear from God.

HOW TO GET STARTED

Here's an example: if your whole congregation needs to come together around a building project, walk through the following questions with your board and then with the whole church during worship, including people under eighteen. Here are questions you can ask:

▦ Who does God want us to minister to in this building?

▦ What does God want us to do in this building to further his kingdom? Have kids draw what they think God wants the building to look like.

▦ When does God want us to take action?

▦ Where does God want us to start?

▦ Why does God want us to do a building project?

▦ How does God want us to pull this off?

Be creative. God has this. Engage with him. Help others get present with God. Ask God good questions. Allow yourself to rewrite, and morph questions so that the group you're leading can ask God the specific questions they have.

You also can use this process as you're seeking the Lord's guidance in your personal life. For example, ask, "What college should I attend?" or "Should I take this new job?" or "Should we move?" Try the who-what-when-where-why-how questions, and see what works. Notice how God is moving and shaping your life as you ask him to speak into decisions. Don't just decide.

When we ask questions of God, it helps us get out of our self-focused way of thinking. When we're willing to consider that God may have a different plan than we do, we can find ourselves making a much different decision than we expected. When we ask God to make the decision for us, we find ourselves right in the middle of the will of God. Isn't that where we all want to be?

DECIDING WHERE TO GO, EVEN
WHEN YOUR GUT SAYS NO

When our church group was trying to decide where to go on a mission trip, Jamaica came up. I assumed that the youth just wanted to go on a great vacation, so when we did this process and things still pointed fully in that direction, I was frustrated.

I told the youth as we left that I would see if this was a location where the missions organization takes groups. As we left, I realized that one family had been missing. That night I wondered where God *really* wanted us to go, and I was pretty sure it wasn't Jamaica. I thought, *Jamaica is a vacation destination, not a place where you go on a mission trip.*

After doing this process, I always give the group a few weeks to process what we heard. This also gave me time to contact the missions organization and see when and where we could go. Well, the next time I walked into the youth room, one of the boys from the family that hadn't been there had written *JAMAICA* on the board as big as he could. So I was sure he'd been talking to other kids. As I questioned him, I realized quickly that wasn't the case. I asked him why he wrote *Jamaica*, and he said confidently, "I do not know."

That moment I realized God was showing me one more way he speaks to us clearly as a group. I also knew I needed to put my own ideas aside and trust what God had in mind.

I've done mission trips for more than twenty years, and I went on that one more than fifteen years ago. I grew much in my process of listening to the Lord and trusting him on that trip. And I had multiple spiritual awakenings—not just for me but also for many others who went. God had a plan for us that trip—a plan for *me* on that trip!—and I'm very thankful the Holy Spirit told us where to go, not *me*. And yes, one of the ten days was a beautiful vacation day at the ocean, but the other nine days were a full-on mission trip.

These are the things God has revealed to us by his Spirit. The Spirit searches all things, even the deep things of God. For who knows a person's thoughts except their own spirit within them? In the same way no one knows the thoughts of God except the Spirit of God. What we have received is not the spirit of the world, but the Spirit who is from God, so that we may understand what God has freely given us. This is what we speak, not in words taught us by human wisdom but in words taught by the Spirit, explaining spiritual realities with Spirit-taught words. The person without the Spirit does not accept the things that come from the Spirit of God but considers them foolishness, and cannot understand them because they are discerned only through the Spirit. The person with the Spirit makes judgments about all things, but such a person is not subject to merely human judgments, for,

> "Who has known the mind of the Lord
> so as to instruct him?" (1 Corinthians 2:10-16)

THE SPIRITUAL AND BIBLICAL
PERSPECTIVE ON DISCERNMENT

Throughout Scripture, God speaks of discernment. He encourages us to go that route rather than experience *folly*. Now, that's a word we sure don't hear much anymore. And none of us wants to experience the fruit of folly.

Solomon asked for a wise and a discerning heart, and God granted it to him, because it wasn't for selfish gain.

"So give your servant a discerning heart to govern your people and to distinguish between right and wrong. For who is able to govern this great people of yours?"

The Lord was pleased that Solomon had asked for this. So God said to him, "Since you have asked for this and not for long life or wealth for yourself, nor have asked for the death of your enemies but for discernment in administering justice, I will do what you have asked. I will give you a wise and discerning heart, so that there will never

have been anyone like you, nor will there ever be."
(1 Kings 3:9-12)

Though it's clear in Scripture that there will never again be someone like Solomon, our own hearts must be in the right place to hear from God when we approach the discernment process. Our hearts need not be seeking selfish gain but truly desiring the will of God for our communities.

Part of having our hearts aligned with Christ is believing that God will speak. As we enter into the discernment process, we may be skeptical, but we can't be people who mock God. Scripture says that if we truly seek God, knowledge comes easily. "The mocker seeks wisdom and finds none, but knowledge comes easily to the discerning" (Proverbs 14:6), and "the heart of the discerning acquires knowledge, for the ears of the wise seek it out" (Proverbs 18:15). Being discerning involves listening, being willing to be guided, and reading the Word of God. Proverbs 1 is a great reminder that the proverbs are there for us to gain wisdom and insight. They remind us how to listen to the words and guidance of God.

The discernment process I lay out is only as strong as participants' connection to God and his Word. That's why I offer this passage:

> I urge you, brothers and sisters, in view of God's mercy, to offer your bodies as a living sacrifice, holy and pleasing to God—this is your true and proper worship. Do not conform to the pattern of this world, but be transformed by the renewing of your mind. Then you will be able to test and approve what God's will is—his good, pleasing and perfect will. (Romans 12:1-2)

A few years ago, we used this process with a group of age-diverse people to discern if we should do vacation Bible school

(VBS) again that summer or try something different. We invited twelve people with a high level of investment in VBS to do the process together.

When we asked the *who* question, it became all about at-risk kids and a nursing home a mile from our church. We went from a traditional VBS program to a full-on service summer that involved our whole church. As a community, we were transformed by this discernment process. We didn't plan what we wanted; we asked God the direction we should go, and he guided each step of the way.

The following year, we adjusted, and next year we will adjust again. Just because we asked God how to do something didn't mean we became perfect event planners. But we did see a community transformed by the work of the Holy Spirit.

As we asked the *what* question, we did things that were outside our comfort levels. Because we asked *where* he wanted us to go, we felt confident God wanted us to be there, even when it felt chaotic. God was stretching us, so we kept pushing forward. We met community members we never would have with our VBS program. Our church members took on leadership they never would have if we'd stayed with VBS. As we ask God *why*, we are a part of making a difference locally, regionally, and globally.

It was hard at times, but so is VBS. That's because we asked God *how* to make a significant shift in what we were doing. We asked God as a group, not just as individuals. It makes a difference when you ask God corporately rather than asking God only individually.

When I rewind the events of that summer, four moments stick out in my mind. I told the recreation director at the nursing home that our church wanted to come and serve at their facility that summer. At first he was very hesitant. He was probably thinking,

We really do not need a group of amateurs painting a room, thank you. I pressed in a little more, because I wanted him to tell me what his facility needed or wanted. During the discernment process, God had specified that the facility tell us what they needed, so I knew I needed to press. I said, "We were thinking about something with plants, since you have a garden club. Our church members could participate with your residents."

He replied, "We have always wanted a wheelchair-accessible raised garden."

I could not believe it. Two years earlier, our church had built a huge raised garden for an urban garden project that was wheelchair accessible, so I knew we had the ability. Long story short, there is now a beautiful garden at the facility, not because my church is awesome, but because God is awesome, and he told us *exactly* what he wanted us to do when we asked him those six simple questions.

A few weeks later, we had a community event called BBQ and Books. I and another pastor met a woman fighting for equality in her neighborhood. We were both impressed with her strength and determination. Out of the blue, she asked us to pray for her. As we finished praying, she looked at both of us with tears in her eyes and said, "Thank you. I was feeling so alone." God ministered to all three of us as we basked in that moment. God had come near to three leaders that needed to be reminded we weren't alone in breaking new ground.

God was also calling us to raise money for two different schools in need. One of my crazy ideas was to go door-to-door with flyers, inviting people to give stuff for a garage sale. As I encouraged the congregation to do this, I asked them to pray. I added, "Maybe God will do more than just give us stuff to sell. Maybe someone will come to Christ as we ask them for their junk."

We distributed one thousand two hundred flyers with my cell number on them, requesting that people call after four on the Sunday we were picking things up. I got text messages and phone calls all week. Each time a call came in, I heard hard stories about divorce, family moving far away, and selling houses. On the day of the pickup, my phone was blowing up with text messages and phone calls. At one point, I missed a call followed by a text message desperately asking for a pickup. I told the caller we would be there in three minutes, since that's what the GPS said. I had a teenager riding shotgun, who suddenly wanted to pick up two more teens to help us. We gathered them up along the way.

When we pulled up, we found a woman weeping on the stoop. One of the teens blurted out, "Why is she crying?"

I said, "I do not know, but we need to be nice. Maybe she'll tell us."

We piled out of the car, and I introduced myself. She asked if we could talk and pray together. She and I sat down as the teens loaded up her stuff, and within twenty minutes she asked to start a relationship with Christ. I gave her the Bible in my car, which I'd put there just days before to give to my hairdresser. God knew that woman would need someone to stop by that day.

So God was in charge that day. He was in charge from the beginning of planning that summer. He knew her by name even before we put those crazy flyers on her door. Now, the real question: does the pastor take the risk again of passing out her phone number to one thousand two hundred people? You bet she does! Did our summer honor God? Was it biblical? Did other believers confirm it? Did it bear good fruit? Did God make it happen? Yes, yes, yes, yes, and yes.

LEADING GROUP DISCERNMENT

Get enough paper and colored pencils for everyone, and have them all fold the paper into fourths. Ask them to write "who" in the first quadrant.

Help them pause and connect with God, doing the practice individually. Then have them share their thoughts with the group. Write down areas in which they agree, and then lead them through each of the rest of the questions: What? When? Where? Why? How?

Take next steps with the things God has revealed. Or take more steps in discernment if there is no clear path that God has shown you. Often it takes just a simple step, such as making phone calls, to find out what will actually work.

Remind the group that this is only the beginning. They have just started a dialogue with God about how to move forward. Also remind them that they all want to hear certain things from God, so they need to stay aware of biases that may exist in the listening process.

USING THIS PROCESS

We can use this process for corporate discernment in ministry when planning big events, such as retreats or one-day community events. Usually when we plan an event, even in a ministry setting, we just go through the planning process not really considering what God wants us to do or accomplish during that event. We're so busy in ministry, we don't take the time to ask God what he wants the theme or focus of an event to be. Instead, we take our great idea and assume God has put it in our minds and hearts. Of course, he can do that, and when you do the spiritual discernment process, your ideas will be confirmed not just by you but also by others in the room with you, asking God to speak.

One of the best things about this discernment process is that it takes the pressure off you as a leader. Instead of you being fully responsible for planning, God is. Isn't that what we all want anyway—to start with discernment from the beginning, instead of trying to explain and justify what we've planned? When we ask God first and watch God plan, we are far less anxious in the process. Knowing God planned it, we can rest in knowing he is in charge and knows exactly how he wants it to play out—even to the tiniest details.

Conclusion

GETTING STARTED

Here we are at the end of a book full of
ideas, full of ways you can draw groups into the
heart of God. You may be wondering where to start.
As you think about all the practices, which ones stand out
to you right now? Which practices are you excited about
leading? Which practices did you enjoy most as you did
them? How are you feeling about embarking on this spiritual journey in your ministry?

Take a quiet moment with God, and think about your
group. What does your group need right now? Do they
need community? Do they need to engage with the
Word of God at a deeper level? Do they need to learn
to be still? Do they need to tap into something
radically new, or do they need to do something
familiar? Which practices are you excited to lead, and
which of those do you think your group needs? Those practices
will be a great place to get started.

Find a few easy practices that you can integrate into what
you're already doing in ministry. If this is the first time
your group has done anything like this, start small. Try a

two-minute exercise before you try an hour-long exercise. Try an hour-long exercise before you do a twenty-four-hour retreat.

I've set this book up in an order that can help groups learn one element before another, building on one another. This way groups can slowly grow in their abilities to go deeper and deeper with God and with one another. You don't have to do the book in order, but if you're struggling to know where to start, start in chapters one and two before you try anything else.

A good way to introduce the concepts is right in the middle of a worship service, at the beginning of a Sunday school class, or at the beginning or end of a meeting. After using the spiritual practices in small ways, you'll find more and more people being open to them in bigger ways.

Once your ministry group has tried a few practices in and among "regular" ministry, you can offer something like a two-hour workshop after church, an afternoon of discernment, or a twenty-four-hour retreat. The key is to start small. Build on what you've tried and have been successful at—before you do too much.

I have a group that meets weekly for an hour and a half, and all we do is spiritual practices. I'd been doing spiritual practices with the church board and with our staff prior to this group starting. It actually came out of someone inviting me to lead a women's book group that read and discussed the Sensible Shoes series by Sharon Garlough Brown. The women in the book came together weekly to do spiritual practices, so that's what we did too—and we loved it.

Before you start a group like this, make sure you've done spiritual practices on your own and led a few in small ministry settings. Doing this weekly is a big commitment, so make sure you've done a few smaller things before you jump in the deep end. For example, I wouldn't start with a three-day retreat until your group has tried some of the practices other ways first. Stay aware of your people. Stay in touch with what you think they need, want, and can handle. This will help you be most successful.

As you engage with this new way of leading and teaching in ministry, be patient with yourself. Give yourself lots of space to try something and fail. Remember to tell everyone it's an experiment and that you are also learning as you go.

I recently said to a friend of mine, "If you want, I can come and lead a retreat or a workshop after you've done a few small spiritual practices to introduce the concept. Then tell them I'll come in as an outside expert. After I leave, if they hated it, you can side with them, and say, 'I know, right?' But, if they love it, you can say 'Awesome! You want to try this some more?'" Bringing in an expert for a bigger event could take the group to the next level, but if you try doing the practices in this book, over time you'll become the expert. Do what you know your group needs and can handle, and see where God takes it.

I've found over the years that giving people multiple ways to meet with the living God helps the community find the best ways for them to connect with God. My hope is that this book doesn't become a long list of musts but a true gift of life-giving ways to invite all sorts of people and personalities into the heart of God. Find what works and what does not work in your community by trying, failing, and sometimes succeeding.

Blessings in your work as you follow the Lord in as many ways as you can. "Now may the Lord of peace himself give you peace at all times and in every way. The Lord be with all of you" (2 Thessalonians 3:16).

ACKNOWLEDGMENTS

THANK YOU TO HELEN LEE for listening to my heart for
God as I was preaching and for inviting me to write
about how my heart beats with God.

Thank you to my husband, Rodney, who sat quietly
nearby as I wrote during vacations and my days off for
two years. You are a blessing to me as you have taken
on anything extra that needed to be done in our lives.
I'm pretty sure I'd be living in a rundown, messy house if it
weren't for you. I love you, babe, and thank you for ten years of
faithful marriage—and for reading five chapters in the car
on our vacation to make sure I wasn't turning in trash.

Thank you to my sister, Bethany Dobbertin, who encouraged me all along the way through words, texts, and
partnership on retreats.

Thank you to my parents, John and Nancy Ellen
Temple, who have always let me be who I am and who
God has called me to be.

Thank you to two churches and a denomi-
nation that let me lead and grow as I was on staff for over
twenty years.

Thanks to my big sis, Kristen Temple, who has affirmed me
all along the way and bought an extra copy for a friend.

Thank you to Lori Neff, who is the best marketing
manager an author could ask for! You have become a

friend and a great encouragement to my soul. Thank you for jogging beside me as I could see the finish line. You are a gift. Your humor and depth are a gift to me.

Thank you to Shanna Noel, who sent me free products from her company so women could engage deeply in Bible art journaling.

Thank you to Krishana, who wrote her book first so she could disciple me in her ways.

Thank you to Meghan Bruggeman, Meredith McLendon, Chuck Potts, and Sonja Kelly, who read large pieces of my book when it was in its baby phases and gave me feedback. You are good friends, and more importantly, partners in ministry.

Thank you to Jon/John/Jonathan (whoever you are) Asante-Antwi for taking amazing author pictures of me. It was no simple task, so thank you, my friend. You are a blessing to me.

Thank you to both a group of women who met on Tuesday mornings and two youth groups who entered into spiritual practices with me as I learned and grew while watching you connect with the living God right before my very eyes. Thank you for all your stories and for your hearts that follow God with your whole lives. It has been an honor to witness God at work in you.

Thank you to Sharon Garlough Brown for writing the Sensible Shoes books that brought the spiritual practices alive for so many women in my life. Your four women gave women around the world permission to enter in deeply with the living God.

Thank you to Clint Bolkelman at Adventures in Missions. Thank you for showing me how spiritual practices are transformative not just at home and in the church but also out on the mission field.

Thank you to my editors at IVP, Ethan McCarthy and Cindy Bunch. Thank you for making what I thought would be the worst part of the project into one of the most life-affirming processes I have ever done. Thank you for believing in my work at every turn and for making my work better than I could have imagined. I have been spiritually formed through the editing process.

LIST *of* SPIRITUAL PRACTICES

HELPFUL BOOKS

W**HEN** **PREPARING** **MYSELF** to lead people in spiritual practices, I find these books to be helpful.

THE SENSIBLE SHOES SERIES
BY SHARON GARLOUGH BROWN

I recommend reading all four of the books in this series in order, if possible. They follow four characters as they journey together spiritually. Their friendship starts at a retreat center, where they're in a group together every Saturday for several weeks. In the first book, you get to know the characters in real time as they get to know one another and through flashbacks into their pasts. As you begin to see why they've become who they are, you'll become more aware of how your past has affected you.

For four years, I've used this series to take a group of women at our church deeper in their faith walks in order to experience healing as they listen to one another's stories and let Christ heal. Several of these women have been doing Bible studies for decades. They said these books finally gave them the space to internalize the Word rather than just learn things about the Word. They've found what they were longing for: depth with God and depth in relationships with each other.

The first book in the series has a helpful guidebook for navigating your way through the books with others. I also highly recommend getting the study guide.

CELEBRATION OF DISCIPLINE BY RICHARD FOSTER

This classic is a foundational book on spiritual practices. Foster provides clear explanations of each discipline. From my experience, this book has the depth of information older generations are looking for. Those younger than college age may struggle to engage with it.

TANDEM LIVING BY KRISHANA KRAFT

Kraft used spiritual practices when she was desperate to connect with God and literally trying to stay alive. Her honest depiction of her spiritual life is gripping. Reading this book in a small group while also engaging with spiritual practices can help readers find the right spiritual practices for them as they move through life. The book is both challenging and encouraging. It's a helpful tool because it's about someone using real spiritual practices in the most stressful of situations. People can relate to Kraft's story as they read about her fighting for her life so she can live out her calling from God.

SACRED RHYTHMS BY RUTH HALEY BARTON

Barton lays out several practices very clearly and helps the reader engage with them. This book is especially helpful to leaders and groups who haven't engaged much with spiritual practices but would like to. Our church board used it for an entire year to go deeper as a group, shifting how we were having conversations. Using this book to lead our leaders helped us talk about how God was at work in our lives, how God was at work in our church, and how God was calling us forward as a church.

PURSUING GOD'S WILL TOGETHER
BY RUTH HALEY BARTON

This book was instrumental for us when our church—a group of very successful people—was making a huge shift. Gifted people can go far on their own power. When we shifted from relying on our own thinking to pursuing God's will together, we moved from doing things our way to doing God's will in order to further his kingdom. Our shift took several years, and along the way we experienced hiccups and setbacks, but this book helped us as a church board to shift our way of thinking. Thanks in part to it, we are no longer powered by our power; we are powered by the Holy Spirit, who invites us to be a part of what he's doing in and through our church by using a gifted group of people to serve him with all that we have and all that we are.

SPIRITUAL DISCIPLINES HANDBOOK
BY ADELE CALHOUN

Calhoun's book is an excellent reference to have on your shelf as you integrate spiritual practices into your ministry. It includes just about every spiritual practice you can think of. The author lays out each practice in such a way that if you need a quick reference, they're easy to flip to and even to read out loud to a group that may need more information. If you're starting to integrate spiritual practices into your ministry for the first time, I strongly advise getting this book.

EMOTIONALLY HEALTHY SPIRITUALITY SERIES
BY PETER SCAZZERO

In all of his books, Scazzero uses many spiritual practices to teach churches and their leaders how to live a healthy spiritual life in community. Scazzero goes to the depths that he has found people need with God and one another in ministry in order to live a life honoring to God and one another. Scazzero will challenge you deeply as a leader as well as those you serve in your ministry.

formatio

TRADITION. EXPERIENCE.
TRANSFORMATION.

Formatio books from InterVarsity Press follow the rich tradition of the church in the journey of spiritual formation. These books are not merely about being informed, but about being transformed by Christ and conformed to his image. Formatio stands in InterVarsity Press's evangelical publishing tradition by integrating God's Word with spiritual practice and by prompting readers to move from inward change to outward witness. InterVarsity Press uses the chambered nautilus for Formatio, a symbol of spiritual formation because of its continual spiral journey outward as it moves from its center. We believe that each of us is made with a deep desire to be in God's presence. Formatio books help us to fulfill our deepest desires and to become our true selves in light of God's grace.